W9-BKS-950

KIDS' INCREDIBLE FISHING STORIES

By Shaun Morey

Illustrations by Elwood Smith

WORKMAN PUBLISHING • NEW YORK

Library of Congress Cataloging-in-Publication Data
Morey, Shaun
Kids' incredible fishing stories / by Shaun Morey ; illustrations by Elwood Smith.
p. cm.
Summary: True stories of spectacular catches made by "kids."
ISBN 0-7611-0450-X
1. Fishing—Anecdotes—Juvenile literature. [1. Fishing—Anecdotes.]
I. Smith, Elwood H., 1941-   ill. II. Title.
SH445.M64 1996
799.1—dc20   96-6002
CIP
AC

Workman books are available at special discounts when purchased in bulk
for premiums and sales promotions as well as for fundraising or educational use.
Special editions can also be created to specification.
For details, contact the Special Sales Director at the address below.

Workman Publishing Company, Inc.
708 Broadway
New York, NY 10003-9555

Manufactured in the United States of America
First printing May 1996

10 9 8 7 6 5 4 3 2 1

ACKNOWLEDGMENTS

I am deeply grateful to those who helped me locate many of these talented young anglers: Mike Leech and Stephany Wilken of the International Game Fish Association, John Spence of the Billfish Foundation, Susan Baker of the MET Fishing Tournament, and Dave Precht of Bass Master. Much gratitude to Brooks Morris, Dan Hart, Tom and Allison Gillett, Breck Furnish, Charles Powell, Ron Schara, Mike Leggett, Scott Richardson, Luke Giles and the Gulf Coast Conservation Association, Rod Collett, Tom Pettengill, Michael McKeon and the New York Department of Environmental Conservation, Frank Fowler, Rick Attig, Ted Fies and Catherine Hendrix and Zebco.

Endless thanks to Dale Gullicksen, the original desktop publisher, my Baja buddy and fish fact researcher Winston Warr III, editor extraordinaire Lynn Brunelle and my ingenious publisher, Peter Workman, who believed in me and built so creatively on my piscatorial dreams.

And finally, to my mother, Patti, who took me fishing for sailfish before I was born and placed a fishing rod in my hands as soon as I could walk. She truly is the best mother in the world.

Courtesy Shaun Morey

*For Connor Patrick Morey,
a 10-pound 3-ounce keeper!*

CONTENTS

INTRODUCTION

FIERCE AND FANTASTIC FISH

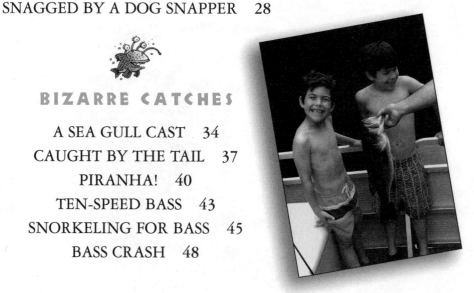

BIZARRE CATCHES

AWESOME ANGLERS

RECORD BREAKERS

INTRODUCTION

Rotted cheese balls, dried-up worms, clumps of sticky marshmallows—these are a few of the things that live in my tackle box. They live next to kernels of moldy corn, smushed salmon eggs and lumps of stale bread. Old fishing line, broken lures and rusty hooks live there, too. Dried lake weed and moss hang from the trays. The box is messy and dirty, and it stinks. I like it that way. When I open it, all that gunk, all those smells remind me of the places I've fished.

When I open my tackle box, I smell lake mud and ducks. I remember rivers and streams and old creaky piers. I think of digging my fingers through Styrofoam cups full of squirming bloodworms, jars of stinkbait and slippery catfish. I can smell the chunks of liver dripping with slime—I'd have to wrap them with rubber bands to keep them on my hook. I think about bass and trout, crappie and sunfish. I want to wipe fish slime on my jeans and thread shiners onto hooks.

But most of all, my messy tackle box reminds me of that sound—that beautiful sound that jolts the heart of every fisherman—the sound of a strike. Zipppppppppppppp! The rod slumps, the reel buzzes, and line spills through the rod guides and dives into the water. The fight is on.

This book is about kids who know about that fight. Kids like 8-year-old David White, who landed the world's largest steelhead; 13-year-old Momi Bean, who single-handedly caught a 925-pound marlin; and 11-year-old Richie Luciviero, who caught a piranha. There are fly-fishing kids, record-breaking kids, and kids who have caught the craziest things.

Every kid should catch a fish. If you're a grown-up, take a kid fishing. Teach him or her to bait a hook, how to tie a knot and how to cast. If you're a kid, teach a friend. And when something exciting happens to you or someone you know, drop me a line and tell me what you caught. It just might be the next Incredible Fishing Story.

Go fishing. Be smart about the fish you catch. Release the little ones and eat the ones you take home. And remember, it isn't about whether you catch a fish or not, it's about the stories you tell at the end of the day.

Fisherman's luck always,

Shaun Morey

FIERCE AND FANTASTIC FISH

STANDING UP TO A 315-POUND TUNA

A 300-pound yellowfin tuna is a prize many anglers spend a lifetime seeking. Known as a "3," the big tuna is uncommonly powerful and can quickly spool a large reel in a run toward the ocean floor. Most anglers never catch a 3. Eleven-year-old Clayton Ludington is one of the exceptions.

Clayton and his dad boarded the 115-foot fishing boat *Royal Polaris* in San Diego, California, for a 17-day fishing trip bound for Clarion Island, a fish-rich island located 500 miles south of Cabo San Lucas, Mexico.

"THE STRIKING TUNA SURGED AWAY FROM THE BOAT, WHIRLING THE FREE-SPOOLING REEL AND BURNING CLAYTON'S THUMB AS HE PRESSED DOWN TO AVOID A TANGLE."

Courtesy Clayton Ludington

The fishing stops along the way were productive, and Clayton had caught a bagful of football-size tuna and large wahoo as well as a sailfish by the time they arrived at Clarion Island.

"When we got to Clarion," Clayton remembers, "I went and got a rod out of the rack, pinned on a pretty big *caballito* baitfish and cast it out. The tuna were biting, and after about 15-minutes the *caballito* really started swimming. I knew something was chasing my bait. I had about 100 yards of line out when the big fish finally hit."

The striking tuna surged away from the boat, whirling the free-spooling reel and burning Clayton's thumb as he pressed down to avoid a tangle. Clayton quickly locked the drag and set the hook. The fish swam deep, taking line fast. For

Many people spend a lifetime trying to catch a fish as big as 11-year-old Clayton Ludington's 315-pound yellowfin tuna.

10 minutes, Clayton struggled to hold the tuna's weight. His only aid was his stand-up rod belt, which kept the pole steady. His arms and hands were tiring fast. He gave the pole to Brian, one of

the deckhands, and grabbed his harness. After the reel was clipped in place, Clayton could lean back without holding the rod. It made it easier, but not much. This was a big fish.

The tuna fought strongly, taking out line again and again. Clayton stood fast on the deck, occasionally leaning the rod against the rail to rest his muscles. An hour and 10 minutes after the strike, the fish tired. Its dark oval shape appeared beneath the water as it was reeled closer to the boat. The deckhand hollered for extra gaffs. It was the largest tuna Clayton had ever seen.

"It took five gaffs to land the tuna," Clayton says, "and a bunch of deckhands to lift it over the railing. I couldn't believe how big it was."

Back on the dock in San Diego the fish was officially weighed. It registered 315 pounds on the scale and was one of the largest fish of the trip.

"It was an incredible catch," remarked Captain Frank LoPreste, owner of the *Royal Polaris*. "Clayton is an exceptionally tough 11-year-old fisherman. He hung in there and landed what will probably turn out to be the greatest fish of his life."

SLIME!

Fish are slimy for a reason. A slippery coating protects the fish against parasites and fungus. It keeps body fluids in and fresh water and salt water out. It reduces friction for better swimming, and makes a fish slick and harder for predators to catch.

GASP!

300

THE IMPOSSIBLE CATCH

The sun was setting on a warm August afternoon. Waves gently crashed against the sands of Allen's Harbor Beach on Cape Cod in Massachusetts. Sixteen-year-old Michael Mealey and his younger sister, Alice, were on vacation with their parents and had spent the day fishing for snappers and menhaden. The fishing had been good, so they took one of the dead snappers, hooked it to their line, and flung it out near the rock jetty that marked the entrance to the boat harbor. They hoped the fresh snapper would attract a small sand shark or stingray. The sky filled with purplish orange light, and Michael and his sister were talking and laughing when Michael noticed a light tap on the end of the 7-foot surf rod.

"When the rod moved," Michael recalled, "I took it out of the sand spike and waited to set the hook. It wasn't a very big strike, so I thought it was probably a small shark. I was holding the pole, waiting for the next nibble, when I felt a big hit. I yanked back and set the hook, and about 10 seconds later the fish jumped. It was big, but because it was getting dark, I couldn't see what kind of fish it was.

"Allen's Harbor Beach is a sandy spot near the local boat harbor. There's a rock jetty that protects the harbor from waves and forms an entrance for the boats. My fish darted away from the beach and swam toward these jagged rocks at the edge of the harbor entrance. It was low tide and I was barefoot, and I had to run across the slippery rocks to follow the fish. It was swimming fast and had already turned into the boat entrance. My fishing line was bent around the post of one of the warning lights at the entrance to the harbor, and I thought for sure that the line would just snap.

"Luckily, I got the fishing rod around the warning light before the line broke. I fought the fish from there for about 20 minutes. It jumped once near the rocks and then took off across the channel into deeper water. The fish sprinted all the way to the other side of the channel, and Alice and I had to shout at the boats coming in and out of the harbor asking them not to cross the line.

"I YANKED BACK AND SET THE HOOK, AND ABOUT 10 SECONDS LATER THE FISH JUMPED. IT WAS BIG, BUT BECAUSE IT WAS GETTING DARK, I COULDN'T SEE WHAT KIND OF FISH IT WAS."

"Boats stopped in the channel and the passengers watched and cheered for us. Other boats carefully navigated around the fishing line. I put as much pressure as I could on the 15-pound test fishing line. My reel had only 150 yards of line on it, and the fish had nearly spooled me more than once.

"I knew I really had to crank to keep the fish from taking all the line. After about 20 minutes I got it very close to shore, but when it hit the surf, it turned and bolted back to sea, taking all the line out again in one fast run.

"As the fight continued, I felt the fish slowly give in. More boats had stopped in the channel, and on the beach more than 60 people gathered to watch.

"The sharp rocks were covered with slippery seaweed. I kept falling. My knees were bleeding badly from all the falls I had taken. This nice woman who was vacationing from Germany followed me and bandaged my cuts with pieces of a torn T-shirt. My feet were killing me, too. They were cut so badly that I couldn't even walk for 3 days after the fight.

"The battle continued for an hour and 10 minutes before the mystery fish quit pulling against my line. I reeled steadily until the large dark shadow slid into the shallow water. Then I waded into the surf and reached down into the water with a gaff Alice had borrowed from a neighbor.

"I was waist-deep in the water, and it took me four tries before I got the gaff

Courtesy Michael Mealey

Though tarpon rarely venture far from warm waters, 16-year-old Michael Mealey caught this 52-pounder in the cool waters off Cape Cod.

through the fish's scales. Finally the gaff went in and I dragged the fish about 100 yards from the rocks to the beach.

"I didn't know it then, but the neighbor who had loaned Alice the gaff had called our parents. As I got the fish to the beach, Mom and Dad drove up. My dad was shocked to see what it was. It was a tarpon, and catching tarpon on Cape Cod was unheard of.

"I iced that fish overnight, and the following morning it was weighed and measured. The tarpon weighed 52 pounds and measured 5 feet long. It was the first tarpon ever caught by rod and reel on Cape Cod. The catch was so rare that the only previous record of a tarpon that far north was one snared in a net in 1915. Woods Hole Oceanographic Institution, a world-famous fish research facility, was informed of the unusual catch.

"Alice and I caught that fish 11 years ago. Since then I've spent a lot of time in Florida trying to catch another tarpon. Florida is known for its tarpon, but to this day I have never landed a tarpon down there. I guess I have better luck catching tarpon in places where there aren't supposed to be any."

FAVORITE FISHES' FAVORITE FOODS

- **Catfish and carp love bread.**
- **Perch and sunfish are drawn to stinky cheese chunks.**
- **Chub and catfish have a hankering for hot dogs and leftover lunchmeats.**
- **Largemouth bass like minnows and night-crawlers, while small-mouth bass prefer crickets.**

REEL-BREAKING CARP

As Cougar Elfervig stood on the long, sun-bleached wooden dock at Lake Powell, Utah, he knew exactly what he was doing. At age 7, he was an experienced fisherman, and at Lake Powell he had caught buckets of carp.

Lake Powell is an enormous lake with towering cliffs, barren beaches and a few cacti scattered about its rocky hills. Cougar was spending a week fishing the lake with his family aboard their houseboat. The fishing had been excellent that week, so Cougar's parents entered him in the monthly Carp and Catfish Contest for kids under the age of 14.

"I was fueling our boat and watching Cougar chum

the water with bread," his dad says. "He was trying to get the carp to come to the surface to feed. A few fish came up, and then he saw a big fish swim by. He tossed out a breaded hook and the fish took it.

Courtesy Cougar Elfervig

Seven-year-old Cougar Elfervig holds one of his favorite fishes—a large, feisty trout.

"It was a big carp, and it almost yanked him off the pier. But Cougar held on, and he started hollering for me to come help him with his fish. But I couldn't. I had to tell him that it was his

fish and he was in a tournament so nobody could help him. I told him he was doing everything right. I knew he was a good enough fisherman to land that fish."

Cougar struggled to hold the thick-bodied carp, and after a few minutes he knelt on the pier and wedged his fishing

THEN SOMETHING INSIDE THE SMALL PLASTIC REEL SNAPPED. THE TIRED FISH HOVERED ON THE SURFACE JUST OUT OF REACH, BUT COUGAR COULD NOT TURN THE REEL.

rod in one of the metal cleats used to tie off boats. The cleat looked like a two-stemmed T, and the rod fit snugly beneath the bar of the T. Then Cougar laid his body across the rod and the cleat and waited for the carp to slow its run.

"I was amazed at how creative he was. The fish was so big and Cougar was using an inexpensive little plastic rod. I didn't think the line would hold, but it did."

The carp tired and turned back toward the pier. Cougar slid the rod out of the cleat and stood up. The fish was strong and stubborn, and Cougar strained against its weight, almost tumbling into the water a few times. A crowd gathered nearby to watch. Boats pulled alongside the fuel dock, and everyone aboard stopped to clap and cheer for Cougar.

Concerned that he might fall off the dock, Cougar's mother and older sister joined him, and though they didn't help him reel in the fish, his mom held his waist and his sister held his mother's waist. The three of them stood single file on the fuel dock as Cougar raised and lowered the fishing rod and slowly retrieved the line.

"Twenty minutes passed," his dad continues with eyes sparkling with pride, "before the fish was within reach." Then something inside the small plastic reel snapped. The tired fish hovered on the surface just out of reach, but Cougar could not turn the reel. He dropped the fishing pole and took the line in his bare hands and pulled the heavy carp to the dock. Cougar's mom took the net, reached over the side of the dock, and scooped most of the fish into the net.

The carp was larger than the net! It was a huge fish. When the fish finally hit the dock nobody could believe it was caught by such a young kid with a dimestore rod and reel.

The fish weighed 32 pounds, enough to win Cougar the contest and the 25-dollar prize.

Some weeks later, Wayne Gustavison of the Utah Fish and Game Department called Cougar and his dad to confirm the rumor that Cougar had caught a 32-pound carp. Wayne told them that if the scales at the dock were accurate, Cougar would be the holder of the new carp state record.

Wayne certified the scales and interviewed the store employees who had seen and weighed the fish. Then he called and congratulated Cougar on his record catch.

Since nobody thought it was a record when he caught it, no photographs had been taken of Cougar's carp. But Cougar remembers exactly how big the fish was. "It was fat all the way around!" he tells everyone.

Most fish never sleep.

BIG BUFFALO

"That's the biggest fish I've ever seen!" cried 11-year-old John Mills, in the darkness to his uncles. "I think it's a channel catfish . . . no, look at its head . . . it's gotta be a carp! Wait! I don't know . . . Whatever it is, it's *huge!*"

John and his uncles stood at the edge of Lake Pomme de Terre, one of Missouri's most popular fishing spots. They were celebrating the Fourth of July weekend at a campground near the lake's shore. The sun had set a few hours earlier, and except for the occasional pop of a firecracker, the warm night air was calm and quiet.

The fishing had been slow all night. At about 10:30, John baited his hook with bloodbait and tried to attract some of the lake's lunker catfish. The fish just nibbled at John's bait. Each time his fishing rod bounced, he picked it up, felt nothing and reeled in slack line. Frustrated by the bait-stealing fish, John rebaited his hook and cast his line far into the lake. He set the rod on a log and waited.

Suddenly, something grabbed his bait. John reared back to set the hook. The fish swung its head, swam to the surface and rolled. Then it sank to the bottom and grudgingly came toward

Courtesy John Mills

This monster buffalo weighed 21 pounds. 11-year-old John Mills landed it using 10-pound fishing line.

shore. It fought sluggishly as it neared the bank, then suddenly turned and charged back to deeper water.

"I think it's going to come up again!" John exclaimed. John's uncle grabbed a flashlight from his tackle box and shined it on the water. The large fish surfaced a second time, and in the light John saw a huge, dingy yellow-colored head with broad scales.

"THAT'S NO CATFISH!"

"That's no catfish! Keep the flashlight on him if you can," John said as he struggled to hold the fish steady. For 10 minutes the heavy fish fought. Then John finally eased it into the shallow water. "Wow, it's a buffalo!" he stammered.

The unusual, carplike buffalo fish weighed 21 pounds. It was the largest buffalo any of them had ever seen. John stored his catch overnight and the next day took it to the local bait shop, where it was put on display. It was an impressive catch not only because of the buffalo's mammoth size but also because John had caught it using the original 10-pound fishing line that came with his reel.

"I still can't believe how big that fish was. Most of the time buffaloes are caught by accident. Nobody really tries to catch them because they're such picky eaters. But I'd be glad to catch another buffalo like that. That fish was huge."

FIN FACTS

WHAT'S IN A NAME?
Some fish are named after animals: ratfish, dogfish, cownose ray, butterfly ray, smoothhound shark, cat shark, zebra shark, dragonfish, lizardfish and hog sucker.
Others are named for what they look like: barndoor skate, shovelnose guitarfish, kitefin shark, bignose shark, paddlefish, goblin shark, knifefish, hatchetfish, milkfish and flathead minnow.
And still others are named for how they act: numbfish, crampfish, mudfish, stoneroller, weatherfish and upside-down fish.

LARGER-THAN-LIFE SALMON

"Sure!" 6-year-old Colby Mills said when her dad asked if she wanted to go fishing for salmon. It had been a month since she caught her first fish, a 10-inch rainbow trout. "If salmon fishing is anything like trout fishing, I'm in!" she hollered, as she ran to gather her fishing tackle.

Colby was spending a week in the Alaskan wilderness with her parents, exploring the countryside where she was born and visiting friends. They stayed near the Kenai, a world-famous salmon river. The Alaskan summer sun shined brightly far into the night, and the land was alive with flowers, lush grass and thick-leafed trees. Animals, asleep for most of the winter, roamed the hillsides in search of food. And salmon, fat from a winter at sea feasting on sardines and anchovies, charged the rivers to spawn and die.

At midday on July 18, 1995, Colby and her family boarded a small fishing boat and motored out from the riverbank with salmon guide Joe Hanes. The fishing lines were rigged with bait and set out behind the boat, which slowly drifted downcurrent.

After about an hour, Colby hooked a salmon and fought it all the way to the boat before it threw the hook.

"That's why they call it fishing rather than catching," Joe told her to cheer her up.

After a short time, Colby's fishing line stretched tight and her pole slammed down and curled under. Colby stood and set the hook. The fish was strong, and Colby struggled to keep her balance in the small boat. Joe was worried that his young angler would be hauled overboard by the large salmon, so he held her waist with one arm and steadied the rod with the other.

This giant salmon outweighed Colby by 24 pounds.

The salmon rushed away and Colby waited patiently for it to finish its first hard run. Then she pulled at the fish with all her strength. She reeled when she could to keep the fishing line from going slack. Joe gave her encouragement and coached her through the fight. He also tightened the drag in hopes of tiring the big fish before Colby's strength gave

COLBY'S FISHING LINE STRETCHED TIGHT AND HER POLE SLAMMED DOWN AND CURLED UNDER.

out. She was determined. She held the rod steady and never gave up.

The fight went on for 40 minutes. The fish had jumped three times and it was large. But when the fish was finally hauled in beside the boat, everyone was shocked. It was enormous, much too long to fit into the net nose first, so Joe decided to wait for a better chance. The fish swam off a little way, and a few minutes later Colby brought it in sideways and Joe netted it.

The salmon was safely stowed, and later that afternoon it was weighed and measured at the shore. It stretched 52

inches from head to tail and weighed 76 pounds. Colby also measured 52 inches, from head to toe, but she weighed only 52 pounds. The salmon was one of the largest caught that year, and it had been landed by one of the youngest anglers on the river.

"Slimy and satisfying," Colby exclaimed happily when she first touched her fish, quoting Pumbaa in the movie *The Lion King*. Not a bad description by a pint-sized angler who had landed a fish most people six times her age would envy.

We have eyelids to keep our eyes moist and protected from dirt. Since fish eyes are underwater, they are constantly washed with water so they don't need eyelids.

JACKPOT SEA BASS

The one-day charter boat chugged out of the harbor at San Pedro, California, on a warm summer morning in 1958. Thirteen-year-old Terrie Allen and her father stood on the deck of the large boat, peering out to sea and the outline of nearby Catalina Island.

"My dad and I fished together all the time, ever since I was about 6 years old," Terrie said. "If we weren't on a boat fishing somewhere, we were usually on the Santa Monica Pier trying to catch barracuda.

"On this day, back in 1958, my dad and I were out to catch calico bass. The big boat was filled with excited anglers when it stopped at Catalina Island and dropped anchor. The bass were plentiful in the area, and the bait wells were brimming with the calicos' favorite food, live anchovies."

Terrie searched for a big anchovy, grabbed the liveliest one she could find, hooked it and dropped it over the rail. A medium-size lead weight carried the bait to the bottom of the sea among the rocks and seaweed and hungry calico bass.

"I waited a long time for a fish to hit, and suddenly my pole jerked forward so hard it almost pulled me over the side. I'd never felt a fish that big before, and I knew it was heading for the rocks, so I yanked back as hard as I could to try and stop it."

The fish was heavy and Terrie struggled to stop its run. When the fish

Courtesy Terrie Allen

Terrie Allen stubbornly fought to win the battle with this 103-pound sea bass.

slowed, Terrie tightened the drag and leaned back. The fish stopped, and for the next 30 minutes that fish took Terrie and her tackle to their limits.

Progress was made inches at a time. The fish grudgingly came up, then quickly went deep. It pulled stubbornly on the line and often refused to move at all. The bass swam away in sudden spurts, then hung heavy like an enormous anchor. Terrie's arms tired and

"SUDDENLY MY POLE JERKED FORWARD SO HARD IT ALMOST PULLED ME OVER THE SIDE."

ached, but she never surrendered. She knew the fish was capable of taking her line into the rocks at any time, but she never seemed to get frustrated. She tightened the drag more than she had ever tightened it before, and each time the fish swam for the rocks, she heaved back with all her strength.

"It was the longest battle of my life. It took 30 minutes before I pulled that fish close enough to the boat for us to have a chance to gaff it. When the fish finally hit the deck, the skipper was amazed by its size and radioed his headquarters on shore. He asked them to notify the newspapers, telling them that we were bringing an unusually large sea bass."

Terrie had landed a giant sea bass that weighed 103 pounds. It was the largest fish of the trip and easily won first place in the boat's daily jackpot. Newspaper reporters from surrounding cities arrived at the dock to witness the remarkable catch and interview the young girl who had caught it.

The next morning the headline in the Los Angeles *Examiner* read, "Girl 105 Pounds Bags 103-Pound Bass All by Herself." Similar headlines appeared across the state.

"It has been more than 35 years since I caught that giant bass," Terrie says. "But the day is still fresh in my mind. It was a real thrill. It's still the biggest fish I've ever caught. The tackle company that outfitted the boat we were on sent me a new rod and reel when they heard about what I had done. The rod even had my name on it! But the best part about catching that fish was sharing it with my dad. He was so proud. He was the reason I fished so much, and he's the reason I still love fishing to this day."

GIANT NORTHERN PIKE

The three fishermen sat on the grassy bank and watched their bobbers move with the gentle breeze. Any moment they expected a strike. The fish had been hungry all afternoon, and 12-year-old Joe Miller, his dad and his younger brother had all been lucky. It was the spring of 1991, and the Millers were hunkered down on the edge of Coeur d'Alene Lake, located near the town of Post Falls, Idaho. A single dead smelt dangled from a hook beneath each of the bobbers. The anglers were fishing for northern pike, the fastest freshwater fish in the world.

At 5 o'clock in the afternoon, Joe retrieved his line and

replaced the bait with a fresh smelt. He pitched the bait as far from the shore as he could and propped the fishing rod on a rock. Then he sat on the ground, stared at the bobber and waited.

THE FISH SWAM STEADILY TOWARD THE MIDDLE OF THE LAKE. IT WAS NOT FAST, BUT IT WAS STRONG AND STUBBORN.

Joe had caught many small pike before, and he knew what to expect if a hungry pike picked up his bait. Pike like to eat and run. A pike will carefully take bait in its toothy jaws and slowly swim off. Then, a short distance away, the pike will eat the bait, before moving off again in search of more prey.

"I saw my bobber slowly move away," Joe remembers, "so I waited for it to stop, and when it started to move again I yanked hard to set the hook. It felt really heavy, almost as if I had snagged a boot or something."

The fish swam steadily toward the

Courtesy Joe Miller

Twelve-year-old Joe Miller (far right) knew what to expect from a pike. But he didn't expect to catch a record.

middle of the lake. It was not fast, but was strong and stubborn. Joe strained and pulled, but the fish just shook its head and remained far from shore. Joe was patient. Every time the fish pulled, Joe pulled harder. He never let up on the pressure and soon, inches at a time, the big fish came close to the shore. He had forgotten his net that morning, but when his dad saw the exhausted pike slide into the shallow water, he grasped it behind its eyes and dragged it up the shore. Pike are dangerous to handle, and Joe's dad was careful to avoid the mouthful of large sharp teeth.

"My dad thought it might be a record," Joe said with a grin. "So we grabbed all the fish and went to get it weighed. We had to go to two different places before we found a certified scale. We finally weighed it at Y-J Foods and found that it set a new Idaho state record."

The large pike weighed 32 pounds 10 ounces. It was nearly 4 feet long and measured 2 feet around its belly. It was Joe's first big pike, and he became the youngest person in Idaho to set a pike record.

"I don't know if I'll ever get another pike that big," Joe, now 17, recalls. "But I'm sure glad my dad was there to grab it that day."

CHEW ON THIS

Some fish, like carp, minnows and suckers, have teeth in their throats. Other fish have teeth on their tongues and on the roof of their mouth. And a few fish, like the plankton feeders, have no teeth at all. The sea lamprey, an eel-like fish, has a toothy tongue that it uses to drill a hole in the body of a live fish; then it sucks out the fish's blood and body fluids.

THE 4-POUNDER AND THE 3-YEAR-OLD

It was a pleasant day in California's Sierra Nevada mountains, where the Banner family was vacationing. The family was visiting the area known as June Loop, fishing from a pier on Gull Lake. Three-year-old Jaime baited her hook with a worm and cast out the line. The bait landed far from the pier and had just hit bottom when the line started whirling off the reel. The fish fought harder than a typical small trout, and Jaime struggled to stop its first powerful run. It was difficult for Jaime to reel in the line and hold the rod tip up at the same time.

For 10 minutes Jaime worked the reel and listened to her dad's instructions.

"When Jaime had the fish in close," her dad says, "we saw it roll on top of the water. It was a huge trout, and we were only using 2-pound fishing line. But Jaime was doing a great job and I knew she had a chance to land it."

Jaime's mom and dad cleared the chairs and the scatterings of fishing gear from the end of the pier to give Jaime room to land her first fish. As Jaime yanked and reeled the fish nearer, Jaime's dad waited with the net.

The trout was just outside the net's reach when it took a mad run straight underneath the dock. Jaime's dad lunged with the net but missed. It seemed inevitable that the line would break and Jaime would lose the fish. Her dad told her to point the rod tip down under the dock. Just when she did, the fish came rushing back out. Her dad was wearing a baseball cap, and as the fish swam by, the line wrapped around the button on the top of the cap and whipped it off his head. The line also got tangled around his elbow. Jaime's dad frantically untangled the line from his cap and his

THE TROUT WAS JUST OUTSIDE THE NET'S REACH WHEN IT TOOK A MAD RUN STRAIGHT UNDERNEATH THE DOCK.

elbow. The fish, still hooked and tiring, swam a few feet away from the pier, stopped, and began to roll again on the surface. Moments later Jaime's dad lunged with the net.

There are more than 21,000 species of fish.

"I got the fish that time, but our net was too small," says Jaime's dad. "The fish lay across the top of the net, and for a second I thought it would flip back into the water. Instead, it flipped straight up and landed head first in the net. I couldn't believe our luck."

After capturing the big trout, the family drove to the local tackle shop to weigh Jaime's catch. The owner of the tackle shop placed the fish on the scale. "Your first fish, huh? Well it weighs 4¼ pounds," he announced happily. "And it's one of the best catches of the year!"

Jaime smiled. She had caught her first fish, and it was a doozy.

SNAGGED BY A DOG SNAPPER

When they weren't spearfishing from a rubber Zodiac off Baja California, Mexico, 12-year-old Tim Vermilya and his younger brother, David, were deep-sea fishing.

"We used to go camping in Mexico each year," Tim said. "We'd camp on a beach with a big bay and lots of rocks. The spearfishing was always great. And nearby was always a commercial fish camp where we could charter a *panga* and go fishing with rod and reel."

Tim's dad, once a commercial fishing captain, had started both Tim and his brother fishing at an early age. At age 10, Tim caught his first billfish—a 130-pound sailfish—and he caught it from a *panga*.

"When the boys were little," Tim's dad said, "we used to take them out in our inflatable boat a few miles from shore and let them jump into the water to watch us spearfish."

In June 1988, during one of their annual camping trips, Tim and his family were at a beach near Las Arenas, Mexico, 60 miles south of La Paz. They set up camp and spent the first few days in snorkel gear, hunting for fish in the underwater rocks a few hundred yards from shore. The spearfishing was good, and after spearing a full dinner's worth of fish each day, Tim and his family put away the spear guns and picked up the fishing gear.

"We had seen a lot of yellowtails while spearfishing," Tim said, "so we went down to the fish camp and hired a *panga* to take us out on the water. As soon as we were in deep water, we started jigging for the yellowtails.

SNAP!

DANGER!
DOG SNAPPERS
IN AREA

"Almost immediately I hooked a fish! It swept out a lot of line as it swam fast toward the rocks.

"Our captain put the boat into gear and we took off after it. He turned the boat and sped for deeper water hoping to pull the fish away from the shallow rocks. I held the rod firmly and leaned back against the weight. The fish was strong and almost stretched the 40-pound fishing line to the breaking point."

The fish stayed deep, determined to reach the rocky bottom. Tim's fishing rod bent sharply toward the water, and the fishing line seemed anchored to the ocean floor. Tim's forearms stung. His back and his shoulders ached. But he could not rest or let the line slack. Any slip in concentration and the fish would reach the rocks.

Thirty minutes passed before the line began to give. Tim leaned back and reeled. He pulled up again, and slowly the line continued to rise. The deckhand grabbed a gaff and waited. Tim's dad and brother stared into the water. The captain shouted in Spanish as a dark shape

appeared beneath the boat. Suddenly the deckhand reached for a second gaff.

"When we saw what it was, we couldn't believe it," Tim's dad said. "It was a huge *pargo*, a fish that usually doesn't hit a jig. They're almost impossible to keep away from the rocks. Tim did a great job."

The *pargo*, called a dog snapper in the United States, was gaffed and brought aboard the *panga*. Tim stared in disbelief. He was exhausted and excited. It was the largest snapper he had ever seen, above or below the water.

"It was getting late when I got the fish," Tim said, "so the captain took us back to our campsite. There were no scales on the beach, so we took photographs. Then I gave the fish to our captain, who filleted it and sold it for market. When we got back home and showed the pictures, people told us it might have been a world record on 40-pound line."

World record or not, Tim's catch is one of the largest dog snappers ever landed with rod and reel.

FIN FACTS

Goldfish can live for 10 to 25 years. Lake sturgeon can live for up to 80 years.

Courtesy Tim Vermilya

Struggling under the weight of his huge catch, a happy 12-year-old Tim Vermilya displays one of the largest dog snappers every caught.

BIZARRE CATCHES

A SEA GULL CAST

Not all sea gulls live near the sea. Minnesota, because of its large lakes, is home to flocks of gulls that glide gracefully through the sky scanning the lakes for small fish to eat. Minnesota is also home to 12-year-old Ian Kimmer. Ian lives near his favorite bass hole at Lake Minnetonka, where he, his brother and his dad fish for largemouth bass all summer. On warm summer days you can see them in their small canoe, paddling around the lake in search of lurking bass.

"One summer day in 1988," Ian explains, "the three of us sat in our canoe casting night crawlers. It was around

6 o'clock in the evening, and we were fishing in the weeds for bass. The fishing wasn't very good, and we had gotten skunked except for a few sunfish that kept taking our bait. I put a new worm on my hook and made this huge cast that went way high up in the air. I was using a heavy bobber, and I threw it so high that it never came back down.

"I looked up to the sky where my cast had gone and spotted a sea gull diving toward the lake. It had my fishing line and bobber wrapped around its wing and it couldn't fly.

"The gull crashed into the water and began to thrash about frantically. My dad saw the commotion, and when he realized what had happened, he told me to quickly reel in the line and bring the tangled bird closer to the canoe. As I was reel-ing, a second gull suddenly appeared and plunged into the water, striking the line with its bill. It returned to the air and dove again and again, trying to free its snagged friend.

"My fishing line was tangled really badly around the bird. There were about

"I WAS USING A HEAVY BOBBER, AND I THREW IT SO HIGH THAT IT NEVER CAME BACK DOWN."

10 yards of it wrapped around the gull's wing and foot. The hook was in the wing too, but not deep enough to cut it. I think the other bird was just trying to help its friend. It kept attacking the line until we got the tangled-up sea gull close to the boat. Then the other bird flew up into the air and just watched us.

"As I reeled, my dad put on gloves to get ready to grab the frightened gull. He reached out and lifted it gently, careful not to injure its wings. The bird struggled and screeched, but my dad worked fast untangling the line and removing the hook from the wing. A few minutes later we released the gull on the water.

"The bird had lost a lot of feathers, and it seemed pretty disoriented, but it swam right away and then flew off with its friend.

"I was psyched when that bird finally flew off, but then I stared down at the pile of crinkled fishing line at my feet. I only had one fishing rod on the boat, and with all of the line damaged by the gulls, I knew I was finished fishing for that day.

"'Next time,' I told everyone, 'I think I'll look up before I cast.'"

FIN FACTS

FISHING BIRDS

In Taiwan and Japan, some fishermen use waterbirds called cormorants to catch small trout. The fishermen capture the bird and tie a line to its foot and a leather collar around its neck. The bird then flies off and catches a fish, but is unable to swallow it because of the leather collar around its neck. The fisherman pulls in the bird with the line tied to its foot and takes the fish from its mouth.

CAUGHT BY THE TAIL

It was summertime in Nebraska, and 15-year-old Bob Pollock and his younger brother were standing knee-deep in the middle of Long Pine Creek. The creek was narrow, 20 to 30 feet wide, and hundreds of young trees cluttered its grassy banks.

Bob was spending the summer at the Pines Park and Lodge, where he was learning all about fly fishing from John Kurtz, one of Nebraska's most famous outdoorsmen. Bill was visiting for the weekend, and he and Bob had decided to go fishing.

Bob was showing his younger brother how to tie the

Sanhill Hopper, his favorite fly, when suddenly, 20 yards upstream, a wild flurry of splashes erupted and started coming toward them.

"Wow! That must be a big trout feeding on the surface," Bob said to Bill with a laugh. But when the splashes erupted again and more furiously, the brothers got a little nervous. The splashes were a lot closer and looked a lot bigger than a feeding trout.

Suddenly, a long, long tail emerged, twisting and flopping, from the water.

"It's a snake!" Bob yelled.

The two boys were too afraid to move. As the snake thrashed and splashed closer, the boys finally saw why it was thrashing and splashing. In its mouth was wedged a great big speckled trout. The snake had the trout by the tail and it was trying to swallow the fish whole. The speckled trout, however, was not giving up.

THE SNAKE HAD THE TROUT BY THE TAIL AND IT WAS TRYING TO SWALLOW THE FISH WHOLE.

The swirling current carried the snake and the fish directly to Bob, who had a small expandable net in his waders. Bob snapped open the net and leaned down toward the water. The fish and the snake battled on, unaware of the two brothers standing in the creek. Then, as the snake and trout splashed by, Bob plunged the net into the water and scooped the pair of them.

The trout flopped at the bottom of the net, and still clinging to its tail was the snake.

"We gotta get rid of the snake!" Bob hollered as he followed Bill. "Go grab a branch and let's see if we can scare him into opening his mouth."

While Bob held the net, Bill grabbed a tree branch and hit the snake over the head. The stunned snake opened its mouth, released the trout and slipped through the netting, slithering away into the forest. Bob reached into the net and grabbed the trout.

On the fish's tail were four deep, red tooth marks that were still bleeding.

"That snake must have bit down so hard that it couldn't let go," Bob gasped. "And with the current as strong as it is, that snake probably would have drowned."

Bill laughed out loud, elbowed his brother and said, "Nobody's gonna believe this one!"

PIRANHA!

Every fisherman dreams of catching something extraordinary. Shark fishermen have dreams of snagging a monstrous shark. Marlin fishermen yearn to catch a 2,000-pound marlin. Bass fishermen dream of the world record largemouth that will make them famous.

Each time an angler's fishing line tugs and the rod bends, he hopes. He wonders what kind of fish is hooked and how big it might be. Sometimes the angler is surprised by what he captures, surprised by his good fortune. Very few fishermen, however, have been more surprised by a catch than 11-year-old Richie Lucivero.

"We were fishing from the shore of Lake Ronkonkoma, Long Island's largest lake," Richie's dad said. "The fishing had been slow that day. The sun was setting and the warm evening breezes had begun to pick up. Then something strange happened. We were using live minnows for bait and we started to get some nibbles. But when we reeled in our lines, only the bait's heads were left on the hook. This was strange because usually when we got bites, little bits were taken out of the bait or else the whole bait was yanked off the hook.

"I KNEW IT WAS SOMETHING WEIRD. IT HAD LOTS OF VERY SHARP-LOOKING TEETH AND IT KEPT CHOMPING AT THE AIR AS IF IT WAS TRYING TO TAKE A BITE OUT OF SOMETHING."

"Tiger muskies live in that lake, and we were using wire leaders to protect against their sharp teeth. Although tiger muskies are hard to catch, we always like to be prepared just in case. Pretty soon, Richie's float bobbed a little under the surface with another nibble, but just like before, all that was left on the hook was the minnow's head. He replaced it with fresh bait and flung the hook into the lake.

"A few minutes passed, and suddenly Richie's float dipped under again and his pole bent forward. He took the rod, snapped it back hard and set the hook. By the way that fish was fighting I thought it was a large bluegill. But when Richie pulled it in and I saw it, I knew it was something weird. It had lots of very sharp-looking teeth and it kept chomping at the air as if it was trying to take a bite out of something. We didn't dare take the hook out of its mouth.

"I unsnapped the wire leader, dropped the mysterious fish into a bucket of water and quickly returned home to figure out what kind of fish this was and to show off the catch.

"Richie and I had decided that this fish must be a piranha. At first my wife thought we were crazy, but once she saw the fish up close she knew it was something strange. We needed an expert to tell us for sure what kind of fish it was. So I called a local tackle store and told them my son had caught a piranha.

I could tell they thought I was just another wacko, but they told me to bring the fish in anyway.

"We drove down to nearby Chester's Hunting and Fishing store, and when we showed them the fish, everyone's jaw dropped. It was a piranha and they couldn't believe it. Fred Laeger, the owner, called the local fish and game department and the newspapers to report the unusual catch."

By midnight that night, Richie and his dad were local celebrities. Reporters came to their home and took photographs and asked questions about their bizarre catch.

"Between interviews and throughout the night, we made repeated runs to the lake to replenish the water in the piranha's cooler, which had been

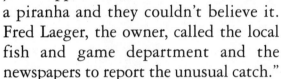
Your chances of being eaten by a shark are 1 in 300 million. (Your chances of being killed by a bee sting are 1 in 6 million.)

placed in the center of the living room. We even put a few live minnows in the cooler. By morning, when the fish and game officers arrived, the fish was still very much alive and had eaten three of the minnows.

"We explained the story to the officers and reluctantly gave them the piranha. We really wanted to keep it in an aquarium and care for it, but having a pet piranha is against state laws. That fish was tough, though. Since it's not native to these parts, it must have been shipped here from South America and discarded in an unfamiliar lake. Then it was hooked by us and dumped into a cooler. And it stayed alive through it all. We had a lot of respect for that fish."

TEN-SPEED BASS

Twelve-year-old Chris Croushore fished almost every day. He knew that the more he fished, the better were his chances of winning the 1992 Metropolitan South Florida Fishing Tournament. The event, Florida's largest and most popular fishing tournament, lasted five months, and thousands of people competed for awards in junior and adult divisions.

One spring day near sunset, when other fishermen were calling it a day, Chris cast his lure into the

Palm Beach Canal. He and his friends had been catching black bass from a bridge 20 feet above the canal all afternoon. Most were small fish, 8 to 12 inches long.

"I made a good cast," Chris said. "And I was reeling my lure in when . . . WHAM! I hooked something big. It wasn't moving at first, so we thought the bass had wrapped the line around a tree branch.

"I slowly pulled up on the fishing rod, and was careful not to break the line. The fish felt strong and heavy. I knew it would be the biggest bass of my life. And I thought if I caught this one, I would probably win the tournament.

"I MADE A GOOD CAST AND WAS REELING MY LURE IN WHEN . . . WHAM! I HOOKED SOMETHING BIG."

"Then it suddenly started moving again. It was twirling all over in the water and I knew it was huge. I was only using 6-pound test, and I thought the line would snap. Luckily, the line held, but something was different about the way the fish acted. It was really heavy, but it didn't fight like a bass. It moved strangely, the tugs on the line were slow and heavy, and the fish never pulled out any line.

"After about 10 minutes, I had it near the top. It was close to the bank and coming up slowly. Then finally we saw it. But it wasn't a bass, it was a bike!

"My friend was also fishing from the bridge, and he started hollering when he saw the bike. He ran from the bridge to the bank of the canal yelling, 'That's my bike! That's my bike!'

"We all ran down to the water to see the bike. It was covered with mud and weeds, but my friend knew it was his. It had been stolen three weeks before!

"Even though I ended up winning the tournament for real, everyone talked most about me catching that bike. I think it was one of the weirdest things anybody's ever caught around here. I know it's the weirdest thing I've ever caught.

"I was happy to get my friend's bike back for him, but I still wish that bike had been a big old bass."

SNORKELING FOR BASS

When they were kids, Frank Rusch and his younger brother, Ryan, spent much of each summer vacation at Lake Shasta in Redding, California. They fished with their parents for smallmouth bass, bluegill and any other fish that would bite.

One summer day in 1982, Frank and Ryan were fishing from the stern of the family's 15-foot boat. The boat had been beached earlier in the day and rested on the sandy shore of the large lake. The sky was clear and the air was filled with the smell of pine sap. Thousands of towering pine trees surrounded the cool mountain lake.

As their parents built a campfire for the afternoon cookout, the brothers baited their hooks with live crickets and began to fish. After a few early bites and not much action, they became bored. So they left their lines in the water, leaned their fishing rods against the side of the boat and relaxed in the summer sunshine.

The moment they stopped watching the fishing rods, one flipped forward, cartwheeled over the side of the boat and sank beneath the murky water. It happened so fast that neither one of the boys had time to react. They knew the lake wasn't deep, so they thought the rod was probably snagged on the bottom. Since it was a new rod and neither boy wanted to lose it, Ryan decided to put on a mask and snorkel and see if he could find it.

Ryan fitted the mask on his face and jumped into the water. He looked down and saw a steep drop-off 12 feet above the lake floor. He took a deep breath and kicked for the bottom.

HE BEGAN TO RUN OUT OF BREATH SO HE TUGGED ONE LAST TIME, LOOKED UP AND SAW A HUGE BASS AT THE END OF THE LINE LOOKING RIGHT AT HIM.

He spotted the rod tangled in the weeds at the bottom of the lake and grabbed it. It wouldn't budge. He yanked again. Nothing. It was stuck on something really big. He began to run out of breath so he tugged one last time, looked up and saw a huge bass at the end of the line looking right at him. It scared him so badly he came straight up out of the water like a missile. He almost flew into the boat and his eyes were bigger than his mask.

Ryan scrambled into the boat and ripped the mask from his face. "Big fish!" he sputtered. "On our rod. BIG FISH!"

His hand still gripped the wet fishing rod and a few gobs of lake weed. Frank took the rod from his frenzied brother and began to reel. As the slack line came tight, Frank jerked and felt the fish pull and wriggle through the weeds.

"When I got the fish to the boat, neither one of us could believe it," remembers Frank. "It was one of the biggest smallmouth bass we had ever caught. It weighed 3½ pounds, and to Ryan it looked like a monster from the deep. We nearly lost our brand-new rod and reel over it, and I don't think Ryan has ever been so scared. He didn't go snorkeling for a long time after that. But I know he was proud of that catch."

Baby salmon travel downstream tail first.

BASS CRASH

ost days, after school let out, 10-year-old Paul McGill and his friends rode their bicycles to the neighborhood duck pond near the city of New Orleans, Louisiana, to catch fish. They fished with poles made from long pieces of bamboo. At the end of each homemade rod dangled the fishing line and hook.

One day, after Paul had been catching perch all afternoon, he got on his bicycle and pedaled home for supper. He rode along the edge of the small pond, holding his pole with one hand and the handlebars with the other hand.

"I was fooling around," Paul said, "dragging my hook

across the top of the water along the bank of the pond. There wasn't any bait on the hook. It was just skipping along the surface."

Paul did not know it at the time, but he was trolling. And instead of pulling a shiny metal spoon behind a boat, he was pulling a shiny metal hook behind his bicycle.

"I was going along minding my own business," Paul said, "when something grabbed my hook and yanked me off my bicycle. I hit the ground and rolled once and stopped. I was dazed, but I was still holding my pole. A few feet away, flopping on the shore, was a largemouth bass. And it was hooked to my fishing line!

"I jumped on that fish as fast as I could, just like a cat pouncing on a mouse. The fish was close to the bank and I didn't want it going back into the water.

"It's a good thing I had the fish, because my family didn't believe my story at first. As I told them what happened, even I was surprised by it. I still wonder how that hook was strong enough to yank the fish out of the water, especially since the strike was hard enough to knock me off of my bike. But I was proud of that catch. It was my first bass and it weighed about 3 pounds. That was 50 years ago, but I remember it like it was yesterday."

AWESOME ANGLERS

A FISH
OUT OF WATER

Some anglers are lucky. Others are good. And a few have the exceptional ability to think like fish, to know where they hide, to know what they want and when and how to catch them. Sixteen-year-old Weston Fowler of Lookout Mountain, Tennessee, has all of these qualities. Since the age of 5 he has caught most of the different kinds of freshwater fish native to his home state of Tennessee and most species of saltwater fish living in the waters of South Carolina, where he spends most of his summers.

"Weston likes to fish so much," renowned South Carolina fishing guide Fuzzy Davis explains, "that he's happy catching anything. He's shown an interest in all aspects of fishing and he admires each fish for what it is. And he's good at catching everything. I remember his first tarpon. He was 6 years old and the most determined young angler I'd ever seen. The rod was too big for him and I had to steady it for him, but he cranked away at the reel and brought in that fish. It was three times his size and weighed 100 pounds. It was impressive to see such gut determination in a kid of his age."

Weston won his first tarpon tournament at age 9, then won it twice more at ages 11 and 12. He's won trout tournaments, bonefish tournaments and permit tournaments. He's caught winning wahoo and dolphinfish and numerous first-place king mackerels. He's won spincasting championships and release championships, and he's been named master angler in tournaments for catching more fish than anybody else. And since the age of 14, he's landed 6 world record fish.

"Weston would rather fish than do anything else," his dad says. "He wrestles for his high school and does well enough in school, but all he really wants to do is fish. And he could care less about records. The only time he gets one is when I'm fishing with him, because every time he catches something that should qualify for a record, I remind him to submit it.

He's purposely released more world records than he's caught, because records don't seem to mean very much to him.

He'd rather release the fish."

Weston's most memorable catch was an estimated 1,000 pound tiger shark caught while tarpon fishing with his dad and fishing guide Fuzzy Davis. They were drifting dead menhaden a few miles off the coast of Hilton Head, South Carolina, when the monstrous shark took the bait.

Courtesy Weston Fowler

No stranger to world-record catches, 16-year-old Weston Fowler poses with a record kingfish.

"The shark took two baits at the same time," Weston's dad says, "so I cut the other line and left Weston fighting the shark. We were only using

30-pound test and 125-pound monofilament leaders, so we decided to trade the rod around so all of us could fight the fish. We had it on for about an hour and 45 minutes and had brought it up to the boat when the rod snapped in half. It didn't really matter, though, because we were going to release the fish anyway. The tiger shark was at least 14 feet long, and the boat we were in was only 22 feet."

Now, at age 16, Weston spends much of his free time on charter boats as a mate helping others catch fish. The remainder of his time is spent fishing for pleasure from his 18-foot boat or learning new techniques from professionals on boats passing through South Carolina or on boats as far away as Australia. He continues to improve his skills for the future.

"He's a unique fisherman," Captain Robert Trosset, the highly acclaimed skipper from Key West, Florida, with whom Weston has caught most of his world records, explains. "He can adapt to any situation depending on how the fish are reacting. He's always experi-

menting and learning new techniques. He is talented in so many different areas. Whether it's a fly rod or a plug outfit, he knows what to do with it to catch fish."

Weston has also begun to travel overseas, tracking different species of fish and learning the fishing secrets of far away captains. He plans to go into the fishing business after high school as a fishing guide in the Florida Keys.

"Weston just wants to fish," his dad says. "He learns new things about the sport all the time. It's what he enjoys doing more than anything else."

Fish that live in the Antarctic have a special "antifreeze" chemical in their system that keeps the water in their bodies from freezing.

THE YOUNGEST CAPTAIN

Staci Austin may have been born thinking about fish. Her mother fished while she was pregnant with Staci. When she was 4 months pregnant, she fought a swordfish for 11 hours. She caught various other fish throughout her pregnancy, including a few marlin. "Staci's got fishing in her blood," her dad says proudly.

Staci learned to hold a fishing rod and turn the handle on a reel almost as soon as she could walk. Then, remarkably, at age 3, she became a useful deckhand aboard her dad's 25-foot sportfisher.

"In September," Staci's dad remembers, "she put it all

together. The two of us were fishing in the Pescadores Club Fishing Tournament. We got to our fishing spot and slowed the boat to trolling speed. Staci was used to being up on the bridge, and when I asked her if she thought she could drive the boat all by herself while I put out the lures, she said yes.

"The rim of our boat's steering wheel is marked with the numbers 0 through 9 evenly spaced

around it. The number 0 is centered at the top of the wheel and is used to keep the boat traveling in a straight line. I told Staci to hold the wheel on the 0 while I put out the lures.

"When we hooked our first marlin, Staci helped me reel in the extra lines. She knew that the other lines could cause a tangle if my marlin crossed them. When she finished with the lines, she returned to the flybridge as I walked to the side of the boat.

"I carried my fishing rod and worked my way to the bow where the marlin was going. I was able to stop along the way to put the boat on a straight course, and then I told Staci to hold the wheel and drive while I got line back on my reel. I stayed next to her so I could grab the throttle if I needed to. But I never had

Courtesy Staci Austin

Three-year-old Staci Austin proudly displays a couple of fish she helped land from her dad's 25-foot sportfisher.

to. She did a great job of driving and we were able to get most of the line back from the fish.

"The marlin eventually tired and I was able to stop the boat and return to the cockpit. I asked Staci to use the radio and call the hook-up to the tournament headquarters. She did, and 30 minutes later, after I had tagged the striped marlin, Staci radioed the release.

"It's been great fishing with Staci. She's done so well that this year we've gotten seven marlin together. I think she'll be ready to catch one herself pretty soon."

Staci will have plenty of family competition, though. In addition to her mother and father, her older brother, Geronimo, also fishes regularly. He has caught marlin each year since the age of 9, including an estimated 150-pound marlin at the age of 12. The fish was caught on 30-pound test fishing line, and it took Geronimo 2 hours and 45 minutes to land it before it was tagged and released.

Staci was aboard the day her brother battled that fish. Her day in the fighting chair is not far away.

FROM BUCKETS
TO BILLFISH

The waters of New Zealand are legendary. The mountain streams overflow with fat trout, and the northern coasts abound with record-size marlin. Anglers travel from many countries to catch these grand fish. A few lucky ones, like 9-year-old Jonathan Curin, live there.

Jonathan grew up fishing. He started as a toddler hooking small baitfish from the back of Captain Bill Hall's 53-foot sportfisher, *Te Ariki Nui*. Captain Hall took Jonathan fishing often, teaching him how to cast and how to work the different reels. When Jonathan was 4 years old, he practiced fishing by reeling in his large Labrador dog. Captain

Hall would tie Jonathan's fishing line to the dog's collar and then set the reel to drag loosely. Then he would have Jonathan hold on as he threw a bone across the yard for the dog to chase. As the dog ran, Jonathan gripped the rod.

At age 7 Jonathan caught his first marlin.

"I had always wanted to catch a marlin, so my mum and I planned a fishing trip to the Bay of Islands over the long Easter weekend. Bill Hall was our captain, and for the two days before we left, he took me out in his boat and had me practice reeling up a plastic bucket. He would hook the bucket to the fishing line and drop it over the side and let it sink. The deeper it went the heavier it got and the harder it was to reel up because I had to bring it up through more water. It was tough, but he told me reeling up a bucket was easy compared to reeling in a marlin."

After working against the heavy bucket for two days, Jonathan was eager to catch a marlin. Captain Hall set a course for the Three Kings Islands, located 45 miles from the tip of northern New Zealand. These three small islands are home to some of the world's largest striped marlin. But the weather there can be fierce and the surrounding seas dangerous and difficult to fish.

WHEN JONATHAN WAS 4 YEARS OLD, HE PRACTICED FISHING BY REELING IN HIS LARGE LABRADOR DOG.

"The weather was very good at that time," Jonathan recalls, "so we left for the Kings. We were 140 miles away and it took 14 hours to get there. But it was worth the trip. We saw lots of porpoise and birds, and we spent most of the time talking about marlin and hoping we'd get a chance at some.

"The first day I hooked a marlin and battled it for 1 hour and 40 minutes before I ended up losing it at the boat. I was so disappointed because it was my first marlin and I was really tired after that fight.

"The next day I hooked a second marlin, but luck wasn't on my side. After a grueling 1½-hour fight, the fish came within range of the boat, spit the hook from its mouth and escaped just like the first marlin. I was mad, but I wanted to keep trying."

The anglers reset the lines and waited. The seas were calm and there seemed to be no marlin lurking in the deep blue waters. Then suddenly a marlin spiked out of the water behind one of the baits. Captain Hall quickly and carefully removed the rod from its holder and secured it to the fighting chair. Jonathan jumped into the chair and strapped himself into the harness. Jonathan was ready for the fight . . . but nothing happened. The marlin did not strike.

Captain Hall kept the boat moving forward and the bait continued to trail through the dark blue water. Everyone on board eyed the lines anxiously and scanned the calm waters for any sign of the marlin. Nothing was stirring. Only the sound of the boat's engine and the gentle splashing of the waves broke the tense silence of the fishermen. Then all of a sudden, without any warning, not one marlin but two arched above the surface and splashed back into the water, each charging a separate bait. Jonathan watched, wide-eyed, and hoped for a marlin to attack his bait. When one finally did, Jonathan reared back and planted the hook deep. Moments later, the second marlin attacked one of the remaining baits, and Captain Hall's wife, Robyn, seized the rod and set the hook. Soon both fish were taking line fast.

"Robyn fought her fish standing up," Jonathan describes. "It was a big striped marlin, and when she got it she tagged and released it. My stripey was still on, and it had jumped a few times. I was amazed at the size of it, but I never stopped pulling.

"I felt like I was fighting with experience. Captain Hall was a great coach, and I had learned a lot from fighting those first two marlin. I began to have trouble with the vest-style fighting harness. It was too large on my shoulders, so my mum stuffed a pillow down behind my back to keep the harness snug against my chest. The harness slipped a lot, though, and I constantly needed to have it adjusted.

"Robyn and my mum kept giving me drinks and food, and after an hour I had finally dragged the marlin close to the boat. Captain Hall saw it coming in and yelled, 'Here it comes!' and the fish was dragged through the fish door at the back of the boat. Everyone was shouting about the size of it. They were all shocked. Even Captain Hall said it was a lulu!"

The delighted crew drove through the night and arrived the next day at their

> "AFTER A 1½-HOUR FIGHT, THE FISH CAME WITHIN RANGE OF THE BOAT, SPIT THE HOOK FROM ITS MOUTH AND ESCAPED JUST LIKE THE FIRST MARLIN."

home port in the Bay of Islands. Jonathan's marlin was hoisted up the scale and registered 292 pounds. It was a spectacular fish. Captain Hall beamed with pride over the skill of his young angler.

"I slept in the next day. I was so tired, and my arms ached when I moved them. But I was so excited! I had caught my first marlin. I got interviewed by local

Courtesy Jonathan Curin

A pleased seven-year-old Jonathan Curin stands beside his first marlin—a 292-pound striped marlin.

radio and I was on the front page of the newspaper the next day. I was also on the TV news."

Jonathan's recognition was well deserved, but his catch was small compared with the marlin he landed the following year. At age 8, again fishing with Captain Hall, Jonathan brought in a 450-pound blue marlin on 33-pound test fishing line. The catch set the New Zealand record for that line class.

Ironically, the previous national record had been held for 10 years by Captain Bill Hall, the man who taught Jonathan how to fish.

"Captain Hall told me I was a good student," Jonathan remembers. "But I know I had the best teacher."

LUCKY CHARM

Some anglers do the strangest things to catch fish. They talk to their lures. They caress their fishing lines. They wear lucky caps and lucky shirts. Some even dance lucky fish dances.

But one angler, living in Ft. Lauderdale, Florida, doesn't need any fish dances or lucky shirts. He is 13-year-old Eric Leech, who since age 9 has placed in or won 12 of the 14 fishing tournaments he has entered. He was the high-point angler in three of his first four tournaments and has won enough cash and prizes to make any tournament fisherman envious.

"He has a lot of luck," says his dad, who is also his captain. "I don't know what it is, but the kid catches fish."

Eric's favorite fishing memory came on May 8, 1992, when he was fishing with his parents in the Pompano Beach Fishing Rodeo.

"It was a weigh-in tournament," Eric recalls, "where the heaviest fish caught wins, and the weight limits for entering the contest were set really high. I didn't think I could catch a sailfish big enough to count, so I decided to try for kingfish, tuna and dolphinfish."

Eric and his mom and dad had been live-bait fishing off the coast of Florida and were trying their luck with a new drift over an area named Tenneco Reef. Eric had set his bait deep when the line began to tumble quickly from the reel.

"I stuck my thumb on the line to see if it would keep going, and it did," says Eric. "I was using a reel with a preset drag, so I put the drag on strike and set the hook. The fish was running so fast, I thought it was a tuna."

Courtesy Eric Leech

Eric Leech is shown here with his record-breaking wahoo.

Eric held the rod tightly as the fish made a torpedolike run just under the surface of the water. Eric's dad turned the boat and followed. Eventually the fish's run lost speed. But suddenly, in another burst of acceleration, the fish dived deep, fighting hard against the line. To tire the fish, Eric kept the pressure on the line and pumped upward with the rod.

When the fish got close to the surface, Eric saw silver glinting in the sunlight and thought the fish must be a kingfish. His dad had a small gaff, and when the fish got closer, Eric and his parents saw it was the outline of a large wahoo. The fish was too big for the small gaff, so Eric's mom had to gaff it with a second gaff to get it aboard.

It took Eric only 20 minutes to land his first wahoo. The fish weighed 77 pounds, which not only made Eric the tournament's junior winner but also set a new tournament record for wahoo.

When asked about his fishing successes, Eric shifts the credit to his dad. "I have the very best captain."

And his captain has one heck of an angler.

FIN FACTS

LOOK AGAIN

Most fish are dark colored on top and light underneath. Looking up, a hungry predator sees bright sunlight, so a fish with a light colored belly will blend in with the sunlight. Looking down the predator sees darkness, so a fish with a dark back is camouflaged against the murky depths.

BACK-TO-BACK BOAT WINNERS

Most kids who win fishing tournaments get to take home a new rod and reel or a new tackle box. Nine-year-old William Payne and 13-year-old Lilian Emerson took home much more than that.

In 1993, William entered the State of Texas Angler's Rodeo, a three-month tournament open to all anglers of all ages. Kids and adults compete together, and prizes are awarded for the largest fish of each species.

"I had been bugging my dad for years to sign me up for a fishing tournament," William says. "So he finally filled out the form for the summer-long state tournament and sent it

Courtesy William Payne

William Payne pulls another large fish from the deck of his family's fishing dock.

our rod holders and started goofing around with my friend. Then I heard my reel go off."

William charged to the fishing pole and lifted it from its holder. He yanked up against the weight, digging the hook into the fish's mouth. Desperate to escape, the fish jigged left, right, then down deep to the middle of the lake.

IT WAS EARLY IN THE TOURNAMENT, AND WILLIAM ANXIOUSLY WAITED FOR THE FINAL RESULTS.

in by mail. The very next day, my friend and I put out a line behind my house."

William's house sits on the edge of an inshore saltwater lake that flows in and out of the nearby ocean. Within casting distance of William's backyard lies an artificial reef where many fish gather.

"I'd caught a lot of fish near that reef before, but nothing like the one that hit that day. I set my fishing rod in one of

"The fish was really strong and it took 15 minutes to get the hook in. At first, because it fought so hard, I thought it must be a redfish. They are known for being tough fighters. But as I reeled it in closer I saw it was a sheepshead. A big sheepshead! I couldn't believe it. I'd never caught a sheepshead before."

William and his dad took the fish to the marina and had it officially weighed. The sheepshead registered 11 pounds and gave William the lead in the sheepshead category of the tournament. But it was early in the tournament, and William anxiously waited for the final results.

Three months later, William was announced the state's winner of the sheepshead division. He was awarded a 17-foot boat with a motor and a trailer and became the youngest angler ever to win part of the statewide tournament.

The very next year, during the same tournament, 13-year-old Lilian Emerson was trolling lures with her dad and his friend from the back of a boat a few miles from the Texas shore. They worked a weedline waiting for a billfish to strike.

"There was a lot of seaweed around that

day," Lilian says. "And when we got the strike we never got a good look at it. I just knew it was really heavy."

For 25 minutes Lilian struggled to land the mysterious fish. As it neared the boat all Lilian could see was a mound of seaweed tangled around the lure and her fish. She strained to pull the heavy mass within gaff range, and moments later a huge dolphinfish was hauled into the boat. It was the largest dolphinfish Lilian had ever seen, and she knew it would at least put her in contention in the tournament.

Late that afternoon they entered the marina and hung the catch on the dockside scale. The 4-foot-long fish weighed just over 57 pounds and gave Lilian the early lead in the dolphinfish division.

Lilian remembers, "It was nerve-racking to place first at the beginning of the tournament. My friends kidded me all summer about someone catching a bigger fish. But when I won, it was worth all the worrying and the teasing."

For her catch, Lilian was given a 21-foot boat with a motor, which she sold to start a college fund. The impressive win also capped a two-year winning streak for Lilian that began when she won the Texas International Fishing Tournament by besting 900 adults around the world. Then, at age 12, she landed a 378-pound blue marlin to win a local fishing club tournament.

Because of William and Lilian, the Gulf Coast Conservation Commission, the organization that runs the statewide tournament, decided to give kids scholarship awards for their own separate divisions for different species of fish. Now kids will win every year.

FIN FACTS

Sharks, rays and skates have no bones. Their skeletons are made out of cartilage—the same substance that forms your ears and the end of your nose.

MASSIVE MUSKIES

Built like sleek missiles with sharklike teeth, muskies are voracious feeders that prey on other fish, small ducks, muskrats, and anything else their size that swims. Although they eat most anything that moves in front of them, muskies are not easy to catch. They are not easily fooled by lures or baits. And to catch one with rod and reel takes great preparation and patience. Most muskie anglers spend a lifetime searching for a muskie measuring 50 inches or more in length.

Mark Shepperd has fished for muskies since the age of 5. He and his father spend most summer weekends at

Minnesota's Leech Lake, targeting the elusive, powerful, sharp-toothed fish.

One Saturday in the early summer of 1995, the fishing at Leech Lake had been poor. For 7 hours Mark and his dad fished, and neither of them caught a thing. To change their luck, they quit fishing and went ashore to wait until dark.

IN THE BRIGHT MOONLIGHT, HE SPOTTED A LARGE MUSKIE FOLLOWING THE LURE.

That night, under a bright moon, Mark and his dad worked a spot about 200 yards offshore over a submerged high point in the lake. Mark threw a bucktail and began to reel. Then, in the bright moonlight, he spotted a large muskie following the lure. The long, slender fish swam just beneath the surface and nipped at the feathers of the lure, but no matter what Mark did, the fish would not take the hook. It followed the lure twice all the way to the boat and never bit.

The fishermen were discouraged but not ready to quit. Cast after cast met with no activity. The muskies were out there, but they weren't fooled by the lures.

Courtesy Mark Shepperd

This fish was the largest of three "once in a lifetime" catches. The mammoth muskie, caught by 15-year-old Mark Shepperd, weighed 38 pounds and measured a whopping 55 inches.

"I thought if the lure was put in just the right place, the muskies would go for it," Mark says. "I cast out my lure one last time and started to reel it back when I felt something really heavy. I yanked back and set the hook and knew it was *that* big fish."

The muskie tore the line from the reel and raced into the depths. Cautiously working the rod, Mark wrestled the stubborn fish, struggling to turn its head. Gradually the muskie began to lose the battle and was brought up from the depths of the dark lake into the flashlight beam that Mark's dad aimed on the line. As the muskie neared the boat, Mark's dad dropped the spotlight and readied their net.

Mark's dad scooped the muskie into the net right away, but as soon as that fish was out of the water, it went berserk. The muskie's sharp teeth scraped at the net, and both Mark and his dad were worried that it might chew its way out.

Mark dropped his fishing pole and grabbed the net. Quickly, he and his dad hauled the heavy muskie into the boat.

"It was the biggest muskie we'd ever seen," Mark proclaims. "We turned the boat and headed in, and when we got back we woke up the manager of the

All fish have scales, but some scales, like those of the tuna, are so small they are almost invisible.

campground so he could weigh the fish."

Mark's muskie weighed 38 pounds and measured an astonishing 55 inches. But Mark wasn't finished. The following weekend he and his dad returned to the lake, and exactly one week from the time he caught the first big fish, Mark boated two more trophy muskies. One measured 51 inches and was caught early in the evening, the other was 52 inches long and was caught 2 hours later. Both were quickly measured and released.

"It's hard to believe I caught all those big fish," says Mark. "My dad's been trying his whole life to get a 50-incher. I think he'll get one, because no matter what size a muskie is, its our favorite fish to catch."

ONE ON ONE WITH A 1,000-POUNDER

Captain Momi Bean, a third-generation Hawaiian, was destined to become a professional fisherman. His father and grandfather had both been fishermen, and as far back as Momi can remember, he was on the sea, helping his father catch tuna for the local markets. He learned much from his father and later became a deckhand aboard a local sportfisher skippered by one of the world's great captains, Bobby Brown. It was from Captain Bobby Brown that Momi learned the skills to become a successful big game captain.

Momi has caught many fish throughout the years and has helped others catch many more. Some of the fish have been big and a few have been world records. But of all the catches, the most remarkable was the one caught in 1982, when he was 13, aboard his dad's small outboard boat.

On that day, Momi and his younger cousin took the small boat out 18 miles to a buoy where baitfish sometimes gather. They wanted to catch live bait for tuna fishing. The boys were successful and Momi was particularly excited when he caught a 9-pound aku (skipjack tuna), which he rigged and sent down on 130-pound test line. Then they started to slow-troll around the buoy.

"Suddenly, my fishing rod buckled forward," Momi remembers. "The reel spun with a loud whir, and it was moving so fast it was way too hot to touch. So I turned the boat and chased the fish. I knew the fish wasn't a tuna because it stayed on the surface after it was hooked. When it finally jumped, I could see that it was a big marlin. The reel was set with a lot of drag, so I slowed the boat and just let that big marlin pull us to tire itself out."

Momi's fishing rod stayed secure in a rod holder near the boat's controls. It was a spinning rod holder, so as the boat turned, the rod turned with it. Whenever

Courtesy Momi Bean

the fish slowed, Momi stopped the boat and fought the fish with the rod in its holder. When the marlin started another run, Momi took the controls and slowly followed the swimming marlin. An hour and a half later, after towing the boat and fighting Momi, the fish surrendered.

"The marlin came up with the leader wrapped around its body, so when I pulled on the leader the fish spun upside down. It was tired, but it was still kicking away from the boat. It went underneath the boat and I couldn't hang onto the leader anymore as it darted from the port to the starboard side about midship. I let the leader go and grabbed the stick gaff. Just as the fish was about to pop its head up out of the water, I got the gaff in it.

"I pulled the marlin up as far as I could and threw a big hand gaff in the side of its gills and put two half-hitches around its bill. I tied the rope to the cleat, but just as I finished, the stick gaff spashed into the water and floated away. The fish couldn't go anywhere, though, because I had its head above the water

Thirteen-year-old Momi Bean with one of sport-fishing's most extraordinary feats. Momi single-handedly landed this 925-pound blue marlin from his dad's 21-foot boat, pictured in the background.

and tied off near the back corner off the boat."

Momi worked fast, grabbing a flying gaff and getting it into the fish. Then he slid the fish along the side of the boat and tied its head securely to the bow. It was a huge marlin and its tail nearly reached the stern of the boat. Momi tied the tail to the gunwale near the stern and charted a course back to Kona. He had never dreamed of catching a fish so enormous.

"MOST OF THE TIME A FISH THAT SIZE WINS."

It took 3½ hours for Momi to tow the marlin back to the pier in Kona. Although he had no radio on board, a nearby boat had witnessed the fight and radioed the catch to a local radio station for its daily fish report. The radio broadcaster called Momi's family and explained what had happened.

"My family arrived at the pier and watched as I entered the harbor. The boat tilted to one side and moved slowly because of all the weight. As we docked, my dad was amazed by the sight of the enormous marlin lashed along the outer edge of the boat."

A big group had gathered at the dock and watched as the fish was hoisted to the scale. The blue marlin towered above Momi.

The weighmaster climbed the ladder and read out the weight. "925 pounds!" he called out to a roar of cheers.

The fish measured nearly 17 feet from nose to tail. It was so big Momi couldn't believe he'd actually caught it. That was more than 10 years ago. Now Momi runs charter boats for a living, and he's caught many more marlin.

"Looking back, I realize how lucky I was that everything went right," Momi recalls. "Most of the time a fish that size wins. I'll never forget that day. It was one of the best days of my life."

Fish have a line of sensors called a lateral line along each side of their bodies. The lateral lines help them to detect vibrations in the water.

THIRD-GENERATION FISHERMAN

Ten-year-old Robert Trosset III and his 5-year-old brother, Christopher, have fishing in their blood. Their grandfather, the first Robert Trosset, was an avid fisherman, and their father, Robert Trosset, Jr., has taken part in 108 world record catches and is one of Florida's top captains. The two youngest Trosset anglers are continuing the family fishing tradition.

"I told the boys I wanted them to fish only if they wanted to," Captain Trosset says. "I never take them out unless they ask, and I always stress the fun of fishing more than the capture of fish."

This philosophy seems to have caught on. Ten-year-old Robert not only has fun, he catches big fish. Robert recently beat out a field of 160 fishermen—most of them adults—and captured the heaviest dolphinfish in the Key West Gator Club Dolphin Tournament. The fish weighed 45 pounds.

But young Robert captured his most memorable fish two years earlier, during another tournament. Robert, Christopher and their dad set out from Key West and followed a westerly heading for Boca Grande island 15 miles offshore. Their destination was a sharking ground known as the Mullet Keys.

"We were looking for lemon shark," Robert remembers, "and we were chumming the area near a shallow point just off the key. We were drifting a dead barracuda for bait, but nothing happened. The surface of the water was calm and quiet, when suddenly a big lemon shark appeared in the chum line."

Robert saw the shark come up. So he dropped the bait back to allow the shark to eat it. When the shark took the bait, Robert yanked hard and set the hook.

Two generations of fishing talent are shown here beside Robert's 263½-pound lemon shark.

Courtesy Capt. Robert Trosset

The shark swam toward the key, then turned and headed out to sea. Robert stood at the side of the boat, keeping the butt of the rod tight in his fighting belt. He leaned back against the pull of the shark and tugged hard with both hands as the line screamed off the reel.

For 40 minutes Robert fought the shark. He eased it alongside the boat and yelled for his deckhand, brother Christopher, to get the tail rope and a knife. Christopher quickly gathered the items and handed them to his dad, who subdued and tail-roped the huge shark. The three anglers then towed the shark to a friend's nearby boat and, with the friend's help, hauled the large shark on board and returned to Key West to see how much it weighed.

The shark measured 10 feet from nose to tail and weighed 263½ pounds. It was the heaviest fish caught in the 6-month-long Key West Fishing Tournament, giving Robert top honors in his division.

"It was extra special because just the three of us were on board," Captain Trosset said. "Little Chris was a big help, and Robert had done such a great job catching the fish. To this day, both boys are creative fishermen, and they love the fun of the sport. It's their love of fishing that makes me happy. I couldn't have asked for more."

FIN FACTS

TOUGH SCALES
The scales of the gar are so tough that Native Americans used them as arrowheads. Pioneer farmers covered their wooden plows with gar hides.

A YELLOW-SPRINKLED WORM

Five-year-old Nicholas Stoud rested his fishing rod on the edge of the pontoon boat. The rod stuck out above the farm pond and the yellow rubber bass worm dangled just above the water.

"Just a few moments after Nicholas laid down his rod," his mother relates, "a big bass jumped out of the water and tried to bite the worm. We knew it was a good sign, and from then on

we had high hopes of catching big ones all day.

"It was the summer of 1995 and we were in Susquehanna, Pennsylvania, celebrating the Fourth of July. We all had been excited to see the large bass leap toward Nicholas's bass worm and were waiting patiently for something to happen, but an hour passed and no one had caught a fish.

"Nicholas's older brother, Spencer, gave up fishing and had jumped overboard to swim when Nicholas hollered about a fish. I put my rod down and went to help him. Suddenly, the fish jumped out of the water. I couldn't believe the size of it! Spencer swam back to the boat and helped Nicholas as I got my camera.

"Nicholas and Spencer worked to-

The fastest fish is the marlin, which can swim 50 miles per hour.

gether to bring in the large bass. They were careful not to break the line, and in 10 minutes they had brought the exhausted bass near the boat. Since there was no net on the boat, the owner of the pond entered the water and grasped the fish in his hands.

"SUDDENLY, THE FISH JUMPED OUT OF THE WATER. I COULDN'T BELIEVE THE SIZE OF IT!"

"He lifted the fish from the water and flopped it into the boat. Nicholas and Spencer put it inside a cooler of water. It was the largest fish ever caught in the lake and the biggest bass of Nicholas's life.

"We all fished a while longer but without any luck. We drove across the pond, and Nicholas caught another bass! It was amazing how much luck Nicholas had that day. It was a shock when he caught the first bass because it was so big. When he hooked a second one on the way in, we were really stunned. But the second fish was small and we quickly released it.

"We got across the lake and took the big fish to be weighed. It was a largemouth bass and it weighed 9 pounds and measured nearly 2 feet long and is being mounted.

"When the fish bit, it almost yanked the rod out of Nicholas's hands. He was using a yellow sparkly rubber worm for bait, which he said looked like it had sprinkles on it. You just never expect a big fish to be caught by a little boy who talks about sprinkled worms. But it happened, and we sure are proud of him."

With the help of a yellow rubber worm, five-year-old Nicholas Stoud (left) caught this 9-pound largemouth bass.

AN UNEXPECTED LOG OF FISH

Sangchris Lake in Taylorville, Illinois, is deep, cold and wide. Its murky waters are packed with fish. Large-mouth bass, white bass, crappie, bluegill and catfish lurk along its muddy shores.

Sixteen-year-old Josh Sams fishes the lake frequently. "I was fishing with a friend one summer afternoon in 1994," he remembers. "We were flipping jigs toward the shore from the back of my buddy's small outboard boat. We were in an area of the lake called Hot Ditch, where warm water flows into the lake from a nearby power plant.

"I had already caught and released a few small largemouth bass, and was hoping for something bigger when I cast my plastic shad toward the shallow bank of the lake. I cranked the reel a few times, and then I felt the lure catch on something. I thought the hook had snagged the underwater brush, but when I pulled the rod back to break the hook free, it didn't budge.

"I was sure I'd hooked a log because it didn't move. I was wondering how I was going to unhook the line when all of a sudden the line started to go out away from the bank. At that point, I knew it wasn't any old log, but I didn't know what kind of fish it could be.

"My friend lowered the motor and we followed the moving line. The fish hugged the bottom of the lake and slowly circled the boat. For 10 minutes it stayed deep, then without warning it angled up toward the surface.

"We saw just a little bit of the fish the first time it came up, and we thought

"AT THAT POINT, I KNEW IT WASN'T ANY OLD LOG."

it might be a really big bass. But we couldn't see it very well because it was only up for a second, and then it sank back down to the bottom.

"It kept circling and lurking near the bottom. It took me another 10 minutes before I got it to come up to the surface again. When it finally did, we saw the orange color and knew it was a giant catfish. I was only using 12-pound line, but since the fish wasn't swimming very far from the boat, we hoped to be able to stay with it.

"The catfish was very strong, and it shook its head, rolled once on the top of the water, and sank back to the muddy floor. I pulled up hard, putting full pressure on the fishing line without breaking it. I had seen the giant size of the fish and wanted badly to land it.

"The catfish circled again and

again, as it had for most of the fight. Then, 30 minutes after it took my lure, it rose to the top of the lake for the third time.

"This time it swam right by the boat, and my friend reached down and grabbed it by the gills. I dropped my pole and got its tail and we just flopped it into the boat. It was such a big fish, we quit fishing for the day and went straight to the dock to weigh it.

"There was a small bait shop at the dock, and it had a spring scale hanging from the ceiling. I slipped

Josh Sams (left) and his buddy show off their 56-pound catfish caught on 12-pound line.

Some catfish have tastebuds all over their bodies. A few can taste with their tails.

a fish stringer through the fish's mouth and hung the fish from the scale. But before a weight could register, the metal ring on the stringer broke and the catfish crashed to the floor. I threaded the stringer back through the mouth and gills and tied a strong fisherman's knot. The knot held and the fish was weighed.

"All I wanted to catch that day was some of the white bass that live in the lake. Instead, I got the biggest fish I've ever caught. The catfish weighed 56 pounds and was 4 feet long. It missed the lake record by just 6 pounds!"

Courtesy Josh Sams

BIG BLUE AT AGE 5

When the blue marlin attacked 5-year-old Oskie Rice's fishing lure, his dad was concerned. Oskie was a good fisherman, the best his dad had seen for a child of his age. But Oskie was fishing from a 33-foot sportfisher without a crew, and the only people aboard were Oskie, his dad, and Oskie's 7-year-old brother, Kaulike.

"We were fishing in Hawaii's Kona-Keiki Kids Tournament," Oskie's dad says, "and that morning I couldn't find a crew. But the boys wanted to go, and since they'd been fishing with me since they were 3 and 4 years old, I decided to captain the trip and take them out without a deckhand.

Courtesy Oskie Rice

Five-year-old Oskie Rice (holding the fishing rod) could barely reach the dorsal fin of his award-winning blue marlin. Behind Oskie are his dad and his brother, Kaulike; standing in front is the tournament queen.

"THAT FISH JUMPED AT LEAST 15 TIMES AND WE TOOK OFF AFTER IT."

"Once we were out on open sea, we rigged up four rods for trolling—two for Kaulike and two for Oskie. Kaulike's rods were strung with 50-pound test line, Oskie's with 30-pound. It was the final day of the tournament, and my two little guys were excited to get a fish. We didn't have to wait very long for action. At noon a marlin hit one of Kaulike's lures, but after a short battle, it threw the hook. We kept trolling all afternoon without luck, when suddenly we got a blind strike on one of Oskie's rods.

"When the fish hit Oskie's line, I figured we were in big trouble. Kaulike began clearing the lines while I got Oskie set up in the chair and handed him the rod. The fish didn't do much at first, but once the lines were cleared it started jumping. That's when we saw that it was a marlin. That fish jumped at least 15 times and we took off after it."

Kaulike coached his younger brother while his dad backed the boat after the fish. Soon the marlin slowed and Oskie's dad called Kaulike to the lower deck controls. As the marlin tired, Oskie's dad needed to be free to wire and gaff the marlin. Kaulike had never captained a sportfishing boat alone before, but after quick instructions from his dad, he took the controls and drove. Twenty-five minutes later the marlin surfaced.

When the fish came close, Oskie's dad leaned out and wrapped the leader around his hand and pulled the fish next to the boat. Kaulike ran over and handed him the gaff. Together they gaffed the fish and hauled it into the boat.

"I was careful to keep the boys out of danger," Captain Rice says, "but I was taking no chances on losing Oskie's first marlin."

The three excited fishermen drove full speed back to the tournament dock to weigh their fish. The marlin was hoisted into the air and suspended from the scale. People gathered and stared in astonishment at young Oskie and his fish. The marlin towered over Oskie, who, standing on his toes, could scarcely touch the fish's dorsal fin. The fish weighed 151 pounds.

The sensational catch placed Oskie second in the tournament. He also received an award for the smallest angler to catch the largest fish.

"Both the boys are good fishermen," beams their dad. "And I couldn't be more proud of them."

THE SCALES OF AGE
You can tell how old a fish is by looking at its scales. When a fish is born, it has all of its scales. As the fish grows, so do its scales. Each individual fishscale has a set of growth rings, and each ring equals one year. Count the rings and find out how old your fish is.

STARTER RAINBOW

At the age of 11 years, Maya Sand had fished only occasionally from the shore of a local lake. The few fish she had caught were too small to remember, and if it wasn't for a good friend, 12-year-old Jake Kaplan, she probably wouldn't have fished at all. So when Jake called and invited her to go trout fishing on a charter boat, Maya excitedly agreed.

"Jake fished all the time," Maya says, "and he was always teaching me about new baits and new ways to catch fish."

Courtesy Ann Clinger

The day of the charter, Maya met Jake at the marina on Lake Pend Oreille, Idaho, and boarded the large boat. The sky was cluttered with dark clouds and a cool breeze blew across the lake. The boat left the marina and traveled out into deep water, then slowed to trolling speed so the fishermen could try for trout.

"We trolled four fishing rods," Maya continues, "and we decided to trade strikes so both of us could catch fish. It was a pretty good day—we caught some small trout under 20 inches."

Suddenly one of the rods sagged toward the water. It was Maya's turn to fish and she dashed to the rod. The fish tugged and fought against the fishing line and rushed far from the boat.

Maya stood on the deck and hauled back to stop the swimming trout. When the fish slowed, she pulled and reeled to regain the lost line. For 45 minutes she struggled to land the trout. Jake coached her and watched. The deckhand stood nearby ready to net the fish. Maya was excited but exhausted by the strength of her first big fish.

"When the fish finally came in, it went under the boat. I tried to stop it from going under but it was too strong. Luckily, the line didn't break, and a few minutes later the deckhand got the fish into the net and brought it onto the boat," Maya recalls. "It was the biggest fish I'd ever seen."

Maya Sand (left) and her good friend Jake Kaplan proudly display their huge rainbow trout.

The rainbow trout weighed 21 pounds, was nearly 3 feet long and was one of the largest caught in the lake that year. Everyone who saw the fish congratulated Maya, and the local newspaper published a photograph of her catch. The fish was mounted, and Maya gave it to Jake for teaching her how to fish and for inviting her on his fishing trip.

"Someday we'll catch a bigger trout," Maya says with a grin. "And I hope it's Jake who catches it."

A FATHER-SON WORLD RECORD TEAM

Tom Hall stood in his front yard whipping a fly line through the air. He was learning how to cast and how to make the fly work by stripping back line by hand. He rehearsed how to retrieve a fish by pulling the line with one hand, then reeling up the slack with the other. He practiced for hours every day after school, often with his dad nearby to offer instructions and encouragement. Tom wanted to catch a salmon on a fly, and he hoped to do it at Wyoming's Flaming Gorge Reservoir, 160 miles from his home in Ogden, Utah.

Tom and his dad had fished Flaming Gorge many times, and in September 1991 the fish were big.

After boarding a friend's boat and steering toward an area where the kokanee salmon were schooling, Tom began casting his spoon-styled fly, letting it sink to where the fish were then stripping in the line in hopes of a strike. He was lucky instantly. Something big struck and ran with the line.

The salmon took more than 100 yards of line before slowing. Tom anxiously

HE HAD PRACTICED ALL SUMMER FOR THIS MOMENT.

held the fly rod. He had practiced all summer for this moment.

Tom carefully worked the salmon back to the boat, pulling in the line just as his dad had taught him. But soon the line was piling up at his feet, and Tom knew he needed to reel it up. But instead of holding on to the main line still out in the water, Tom released it and tried to quickly reel up the slack line at his feet. As soon as he released the main line, the

A lucky catch! Tom (pictured here with his dad) holds the world-record salmon he caught on a fly.

salmon surged away, taking most of the line back out again.

Tom stripped back the line several times, but each time he lost it when trying to reel up the slack at his feet. He tried holding the line and reeling at the same time. But the technique was difficult to master. Unable to get the line on the reel, Tom changed tactics. He let the fish take out all the slack line at his feet, and rather than pull it in with his hand like a fly fisherman, he fought the fish by reeling it in the traditional way.

Tom played the fish as if he were using a spinning reel and soon had the salmon beside the boat. His dad netted the fish and brought it on board. It was the largest kokanee salmon any of them had ever caught. It weighed 4 pounds 1 ounce and became the new Freshwater Fishing Hall of Fame's fly-fishing world record for 12-pound test fishing line.

Tom and his dad fished again the following weekend and set another kokanee salmon world record, this time on spinning gear using 20-pound fishing line. And during the same two weeks of fishing, his dad set three kokanee salmon world records, all caught on conventional spinning gear.

"That was three years ago," Tom's dad explains. "Now we hear the kokanee are big up at Wyoming's Strawberry Reservoir. We're planning on going up there later this year to try and beat our own records. But most important, we're going out to be together and catch fish."

NOISY FISH

Some fish are noisy creatures. They squeak, grunt and squeal. Some grind their teeth to make noise, others rub the bones of their spine together. A few fish even get their names by the sounds they make when caught. This is how grunts and croakers got their names.

WINNING BY A "SPOT"

Three long months had passed since 14-year-old Philip Terry, Jr., unwrapped his favorite Christmas gift—a fishing rod and reel. Since the Alabama winters were poor for fishing, the rod and reel remained in the closet until spring. Finally the time came. The air had warmed and the fish woke from their slumber. In the first week of March 1978 Philip and his dad collected their fishing gear, loaded their bass boat and drove to a nearby lake.

"It was my first fishing trip of the year," Philip says, "and I was excited about trying out my new fishing rod. We arrived at Smith Lake at 6 o'clock in the morning to practice for an upcoming fishing tournament. We launched our boat and drove across the long, winding lake to a fishing spot called Dismal Creek. The area has a small cove and a creek with fallen trees stretching out across the water. We stopped the boat and warmed up by working a bunch of different lures around the sunken trees.

"My dad was throwing a spinner bait, and right away he caught an 8-pound 3-ounce largemouth. That's a big fish and I got pretty excited, so as he was taking his fish off the hook, I tied on a spinner bait like the one he was throwing.

"As our boat drifted back across the cove, I cast my spinner bait toward the trees and began to reel. All of a sudden I felt a light tap on my line. It was a very soft bump and I thought it might have been an underwater twig. And then I felt a second similar pull on the line.

"I told Dad I thought I'd had a hit when my line tightened and the rod bounced forward. I set the hook hard and heaved back against the fish. It immediately charged for the lake floor and stripped line off my new reel. My first bass of the year was really strong.

"It fought hard. It tried to get deep and hide in the rocks at the bottom of the lake. Each time I stopped it, the bass would rush up and try to throw the hook. It took me all the way around the boat before we finally got it to the net. The first thing that came into my mind when I saw it was that it was an 8-pound largemouth. I had never caught an 8-pounder before! It was huge!"

"THE MORE WE LOOKED AT IT, THE MORE WE WONDERED IF IT COULD BE A DIFFERENT KIND OF BASS."

Courtesy Philip Terry Jr.

When is a largemouth bass not a largemouth bass? When it's a world record spotted bass like this one caught by Philip Terry, Jr.

Late that afternoon, they carried the fish to the marina scale for a weight. Philip's large bass weighed 8 pounds 12 ounces.

"When I saw what it weighed, I was really happy. But I really wanted to weigh it again just to see if it was a 9-pounder. It was so close. They had a certified scale there, and on that scale my fish weighed 8 pounds 15 ounces. It just missed being a 9-pounder, but it was still a trophy largemouth bass."

Later that evening a sportswriter for the local newspaper interviewed Philip and his dad and took photographs. After the interview, Philip put his fish in the freezer and began thinking of ways to save money to get his fish mounted.

"My fishing buddies would come by,

and we'd pull the fish out of the freezer to look at it. The more we looked at it, the more we wondered if it could be a different kind of bass. I knew there were spotted bass in that lake, but usually spotted bass didn't get that big. My bass had a smaller mouth than most large-mouth bass and it had a burr on its tongue, which is not common with largemouth bass."

A few more months passed before Philip had enough money to get the fish mounted. But he was still curious about the species of bass he had caught. He called the local fish and game department and asked how to determine the type of bass. He was told to look at the first spine of the dorsal fin and the pupils of the fish's eyes. These were always different on spotted bass than on largemouth bass.

Philip gave the fish to a fish expert at the University of Auburn, where one of the fish's scales was examined. The expert confirmed it to be a spotted bass. Philip and his dad immediately con-tacted every person who had seen the fish on the day it was caught. They got proof from the Department of Agriculture that the scale the bass was weighed

on was certified, and they compiled all the photographs taken of the fish. They then sent the entire package of informa-tion to the IGFA, along with a certified letter from the University of Auburn confirming the fish to be a spotted bass.

"My dad and I did all the paperwork for a world record, but we weren't sure we would get it because of all the time that had passed. I even wrote a personal letter telling the IGFA what my catch meant to me and asked them to please consider it for a world record."

Months passed when finally, more than a year after catching the bass, Philip's catch was accepted by the IGFA as the new spotted bass world record. Philip held the world record for 9 years. Ironically, it was broken by another teen-age angler. "I never thought I'd catch a world record bass, and doing it as a teenager was extra special," said Philip. "The kid that beat me must have felt the same way."

A PLUMP ROOSTER

Roosterfish have an unusual dorsal fin. Long strands of skin jut out from the top of its fin like the comb of a rooster. The fish is a beautiful silver color striped with black. It can grow large and is often difficult to hook. Few anglers ever catch a roosterfish that weighs more than 50 pounds.

The world-record roosterfish was caught in 1960 in Baja California, Mexico. It weighed 114 pounds. Since then, only a handful of roosterfish have been caught that weighed 90 pounds or more.

Ten-year-old Keith de Fiebre has fished a lot in Baja California. He and his family have chartered local boats,

sometimes going far offshore to catch marlin, other times remaining close to the beach to catch smaller species of fish.

Early one Baja morning, Keith, his mom, his brother Brian and his friend Danny chartered one of the big hotel boats, captained by Manuel Ortiz. He was the best captain they knew, and they always fished with him when they were there.

The group planned to spend the morning fishing for roosterfish, then head for deeper water and search for marlin. That morning roosterfish were sighted along the productive half-mile stretch of beach near the Punta Arenas lighthouse.

But the roosterfish weren't biting, and after a couple of hours Keith wanted to try something different. "Captain Ortiz," Keith asked, "can we stop the boat and try drifting some live bait around for a while?"

"Sure we can," chuckled Captain Ortiz. He turned off the ignition and waited while Keith, Brian and Danny baited their hooks with live mullet. They cast the bait out into the water and held their reels in free spool, letting the mullet swim far from the boat. Twenty minutes slowly passed.

"Hey, I got a hit!" Keith hollered. The reel whirred loudly. "It's taking line, it's taking line!"

"Let the fish take it, Keith," coached Captain Ortiz. "Wait as long as you can, then flip the lever up on your reel and set the hook."

"HEY, I GOT A HIT!" KEITH HOLLERED. THE REEL WHIRRED LOUDLY. "IT'S TAKING LINE, IT'S TAKING LINE!"

Keith watched the line spin from his reel. He patiently let the fish eat the bait. He had caught many roosterfish before, and he knew it would take time for the fish to swallow the bait.

"Now!" Keith yelled as he reared back and set the hook. "Wow, look at it take line!"

The boat had drifted about 600 yards from the beach when the fish first hit. After the initial run to deeper water, the fish turned and charged the shore. Captain Ortiz followed the fish and Keith kept the line taut.

"I think it's going to hit the beach!" he hollered as the fish neared the breaking waves.

Captain Ortiz reversed the boat close to the breaking swells. Keith reeled fast to keep the line tight and put as much of it back on the reel as he could. The boat plowed backward, waves sloshing waves over the transom.

Keith concentrated on his fishing line. He thought of the marlin and all the roosterfish he had caught the year before. He was a more experienced angler now, and he wanted to do everything correctly. But this fish was different from the others. It was taking more line than any fish he had hooked before, and it wasn't getting tired.

"Brian, help me out, my arms are burning," Keith said as the fish took another blistering run. "I can't hold it."

Brian grabbed Keith by the shoulders and held him steady, but the fish just wouldn't quit. An hour and 45 minutes passed before the fish finally gave up the fight.

Keith pulled with all his strength one last time. The deckhand grabbed the gaff and reached over the side of the boat. He yelled excitedly in Spanish to the captain and jerked up with the gaff. Captain Ortiz rushed down from the flybridge and stared into the water. He turned to Keith and spread his arms wide.

"Muy grande!" he said, smiling in disbelief.

Keith sat in the fighting chair and smiled. The mate struggled to pull the fish into the boat. Captain Ortiz leaned over the gunwale and together they pulled the mammoth roosterfish inside.

"What a fish!" Keith cried out. "Let's get a picture." As Keith's mom aimed the camera, the happy crew could barely hold the fish.

The roosterfish was too big for the fish box. Its tail flopped out one end and its head stuck out the other. The large hook looked small in the fish's mouth and had caught in only a thin piece of the lip.

"We were lucky, *amigo*," Captain Ortiz said to Keith. "If the fish had opened its mouth, we might have lost it."

The roosterfish was weighed from a rusty beach scale and registered 95 pounds. It was caught on 20-pound test and was unofficially the fourth-largest roosterfish ever caught sportfishing.

"We're coming back again next year," Keith eagerly told Captain Ortiz. "I don't know if we'll ever beat this one, but with you as our captain we have the best chance."

Courtesy Keith de Fiebre

Ten-year-old Keith de Fiebre with one of the world's largest roosterfish ever caught.

THE RECORD OF STEEL

When 8-year-old David White set the hook, he never dreamed it would be a world record fish. It was the summer of 1970, and he had been fishing with his family from a rubber dinghy off the shores of Bell Island, Alaska.

"It was around 6 o'clock in the evening," David said. "My two brothers, my one-year-old sister and my mom and dad and I were fishing from our inflatable dinghy near the shore. The fishing had been slow and we didn't expect to catch anything. I had my bait down deep, hoping to catch a giant halibut, but the bait was too close to the bottom and the line kept getting snagged."

David's dad warned him not to get snagged again. Snags disrupted the fishing, forcing everyone on board to reel in their lines and wait while the snagged line was freed. Only after the hook was pulled free or the line was broken were they able to reset their lines and fish again.

"My dad had already freed up three or four of my snags and had warned me that if it happened again I'd be in trouble. He had me pretty scared, but I put my line down deep anyway."

They were trolling slowly around the cove when David's rod slumped over again. The line moved slowly and the catch was heavy, just like a snag.

"I started letting some line out, hoping my dad wouldn't notice. But he saw what I was doing and his face got red. I knew he was going to let me have it. I told him I thought it wasn't a snag, but he could see that the line wasn't moving very much. It was like I had hooked onto a piece of lead.

"As my dad stopped the boat, my line shot off across the top of the water. I shouted out that I had something. My brothers reeled in their lines and my dad shut off the engine. Everyone watched as the fish raced out a few hundred feet, came to the surface, and jumped three or four times in the air.

"It was pretty far away when it jumped, and we didn't think it was a very big fish. Plus it was fighting like most of the salmon we were used to catching. We thought it was just another average fish, at first."

The salmon remained far from the boat. David's dad waited by the engine in case the fish took too much line. But the fish stayed where it was, and David began to bring in the line. David's dad calmly talked him through the fight. David strained and reeled and dragged the fish toward the boat. But the fish was determined to fight the line, and each turn of the reel was followed by a lengthy run.

"When the salmon was about halfway to the boat it jumped again, and we saw how big it was. We couldn't believe it. We got pretty excited then."

It was the largest fish David had ever hooked. It charged deep. It came to the surface and sulked. It circled slowly and took out line in bursts of speed. Then, halfway through the fight, the line suddenly slackened. David reeled frantically and tears clouded his eyes.

"I felt the line go dead and thought for sure the fish was gone. But while I was reeling in the line, I saw this thing under the water. It looked like a surfacing submarine. It was a huge fish, and it came up about 10 feet from the boat. Then it started to glide away—and my line followed it. It was my fish and I was still hooked up and I couldn't believe how big it was!"

David reeled and tugged with new confidence. The fish tired and took less line with each run. It began to circle near the boat, each pass coming closer than the previous one. David's dad readied the net and waited. He knew the danger was great of losing a fish netted too soon. He also knew David was nearly out of strength.

"I SAW THIS THING UNDER THE WATER. IT LOOKED LIKE A SURFACING SUBMARINE."

"My dad put the net in the water and I just sort of guided the fish into it. We learned later that it couldn't see our net.

Courtesy David White

Eight-year-old David White poses with his world record steelhead. The 42-pound 2-ounce fish was caught in 1970 and is still the unbeaten world record.

It had lots of scars on its face and it had lost an eye. That's probably why we got it on the first try. It definitely had more fight left. When the fish hit our net it went nuts. Water was flying everywhere.

"My dad quickly slid the netted fish over the side and into the boat. It flopped around like crazy until my brother and I secured it with our legs. The pinned fish quieted, and everyone in the boat stared in silence."

It was the most beautiful fish they had ever seen, and it was big. The family celebrated the catch with hoots and hollers heard far across the bay.

It was 10 o'clock in the evening before they returned to the dock to weigh David's fish. David's dad guided the boat up to the dock, and David hauled out his catch. He struggled proudly, lifting his fish chest high and dragging it to the scale. A small group of onlookers huddled around.

"42-pound 2-ounce salmon," the weighmaster announced to the crowd. David smiled. It seemed like the largest fish in the world.

Later that night the fish was carted away to a local freezer and flash frozen. Weeks later it was taken to a taxidermist in David's hometown of Seattle, Washington. While curing the fish's skin, the taxidermist saw that the fish was not a salmon as first suspected, but a steelhead. It was the largest one he had ever seen. It was also a potential world record.

The fish was sent to the University of Washington, where the founder of the school's fisheries department, Dr. Lauren Donaldson, confirmed the taxidermist's finding. David's parents then submitted the information to the International Game Fish Association, where the fish qualified for the largest steelhead ever caught with rod and reel.

"I was just a little kid when I caught it, and when they first told me it was a steelhead, I didn't really care. I just cared about catching such a big fish. But when I was told it was a world record, I think I was the happiest kid around."

It's been more than 25 years since David landed his record steelhead. Thousands of anglers have tried to catch a bigger steelhead, but none has succeeded. The catch is also unofficially the longest-standing world record fish caught by any kid. And David, now an adult, still can't believe it.

MONSTER STRIPED BASS

It was midmorning on May 13, 1995, when 12-year-old Devin Nolan's fishing rod bent toward the water of Maryland's Chesapeake Bay. His reel sputtered as the fishing line unspooled. Devin wrested the rod from its holder and felt the heavy weight of the line. His dad slowed the trolling boat and prepared to follow the fish if necessary.

"So much line was going off the reel," Devin says, "that until we stopped the boat we thought we had snagged the bottom. But when I grabbed the rod I could feel the fish fighting, and after the boat stopped the line was still pouring off the reel."

Its first run was long, and when it stopped, Devin strained to raise it. There was no chair to sit in, so he fought the fish standing up. For an hour he pulled against the stubborn fish. Each time it approached the boat it turned and surged for the safety of the deep water.

"I couldn't believe how strong it was. I had it close three times, but each time it would strip the line back off the reel and head down deep."

When the fish first neared the boat, Devin glimpsed it before it disappeared in a sudden surge beneath the water. It was an enormous striped bass. Devin patiently played the bass back to the boat. The fourth time he was lucky. His dad seized the leader in his hand and his friend netted the fish. Together they lifted it into the boat.

"It was such a big fish, we got on the radio and told our friends where we were fishing so maybe they could catch one, too. But everybody on the water heard our call, and pretty soon they were all fishing around us. It got pretty crowded, so we went in and weighed our fish."

The nearest scale was at a local fishing shop. Devin and his dad took the fish and had it officially weighed. The striped bass measured 67 pounds 8 ounces and set the new Maryland state record. It was more than 4 feet long and nearly 3 feet around.

Devin gave the fish to the Department of Natural Resources for research. They concluded that the striped bass was a 23-year-old female that had recently spawned before it was caught.

Today a mount of the fish hangs on a wall in the office of the Department of Natural Resources. A second mount hangs on Devin's bedroom wall.

"The catch was such a thrilling experience, and to set a record made it even better. But most of all, I was really glad the fish had already spawned, because our state is trying to rebuild the striped bass population in the bay. I love to fish, and the more fish there are in the bay, the more chances there are to catch them in the future."

HOOKED ON BLUES

Alexandra Yates and her father fished together often. Every summer they chased bluefish off the coast of Massachusetts or tried for tarpon in the waters off Florida.

In August of 1994, the father-and-daughter team stood at the stern of a charter boat, tossing poppers to a school of feeding bluefish. They were fishing the currents outside Cape Cod, Massachusetts.

Alexandra used 6-pound test fishing line; her dad used 8-pound. Together they cast to the schooling bluefish, jerking the fishing rods as they reeled to make the lures "pop" across the water.

Courtesy Alexandra Yates

World record bluefish angler Alexandra Yates poses beside Capt. Pete Durmer and holds her winning 7-pounder.

"Alexandra got a strike," her dad says. "So I immediately stopped fishing and brought her a fighting belt. The fish jumped and looked pretty big, and I knew if she could get it in it might be a record catch.

"We had carefully planned for the possibility of a world record. We were purposely using 6- and 8-pound test fishing line because the International Game Fish Association had recently set the new line categories for world record bluefish. All of our fishing gear and the way we rigged our lures were also under the IGFA rules. Our first goal was to fish and have fun. But if we caught a bluefish in one of those line classes, I wanted to make sure we did everything right. It added to the fun of the trip."

Alexandra's bluefish cut across the top of the water and leaped into the air. It thrashed and shook its body and swam far from the boat. Alexandra was patient. She had caught many bluefish before and she knew their tactics. The fish jumped twice more, and 15 minutes after setting the hook, Alexandra brought it to the boat and the deckhand netted it. The bluefish

"WE HAD CAREFULLY PLANNED FOR THE POSSIBILITY OF A WORLD RECORD."

weighed 7 pounds, enough to set a world record. A few hours later Alexandra's dad caught a smaller bluefish and set a world record on 8-pound line.

"That was an amazing trip. The fishing out there was really good. The day Alexandra and I set our records, we probably had 40 fish. I know she caught at least a dozen. But we let most of our fish go. We use single hooks and press down the barbs to make the release easier on the fish. The few fish we do keep we save for the barbecue. In fact, we ate Alexandra's world record after it was officially weighed."

Alexandra's bluefish record remains unbeaten, and this year the record-catching father-and-daughter team will be out trying to break their own records.

FISH OUT OF WATER
A flying fish launches itself into the air to escape enemies. It can glide through the air as far as 300 feet using its oversized fins as wings.

STRIKE ONE!

It was the first strike of the day. When 10-year-old Eric Shivers's fishing rod slumped across the back of the boat, his dad thought the lure had snagged on the shallow lake floor. But as he slowed the boat to try and free the snag, Eric's fishing line continued to pour from the reel.

"I picked up the rod and handed it to my dad," Eric says, "so he could tell if it was a fish or not. When I gave him the rod, he almost got yanked out of the boat."

They were fishing at Sangchris Lake near their hometown of Taylorville, Illinois. Eric's dad quickly returned the fishing rod to his son, turned the boat, and with help from from Eric's uncle, cleared the remaining fishing lines from the stern.

"When I hooked the fish," Eric says, "we were close to shore and fishing in about 25 feet of water. That fish wanted to get out into the deeper water, and I couldn't believe how strong it was. By the time we started to chase it, there were only 50 yards of line left on the reel."

BEFORE ERIC'S DAD COULD GRAB THE FISH, IT FLICKED ITS TAIL AND SURGED FOR THE BOTTOM OF THE LAKE.

Thirty minutes after the strike, Eric saw the fish for the first time. It was a large striped bass, and it had surfaced next to the boat. But the fish was too big for the net, and before Eric's dad could grab the fish with his hands, it flicked its tail and surged for the bottom of the lake. Worried that the big fish would pull Eric overboard, his dad held him by the waist. Eric strained and reeled and brought the striped bass back to the surface. But

Courtesy Eric Shivers

The first striped bass 10-year-old Eric Shivers ever caught was a 31-pound 7-ounce beauty that set the Illinois state record.

when his dad reached over to grasp the fish it thrashed free and swam beneath the boat.

"My dad told me to loosen the drag and let the fish take line so it wouldn't break on the bottom of the boat. The line was only 10-pound test and it was rubbing against the hull."

Eric loosened the drag and waited for the fish to move away from the boat. Then he tightened the drag and worked the fish back to the surface. But before his dad could grab the striped bass, it surged under the boat again. Eric released the drag once more and waited.

"The fish was really big," Eric says, "and when it surfaced for the fourth time, my dad reached out and got his fingers in the gills. He picked it up fast and put it in the live well, but it was so big, its tail stuck out."

An angler fishing from a nearby boat witnessed the catch and yelled to Eric that his fish looked like a state record.

"When we heard it might be a record, we were excited," Eric says. "It took us about an hour to find a place with a certified scale, but we finally weighed the fish at Kroeger's grocery store."

Eric watched excitedly as the heavy fish was weighed. It was his first striped bass, and when his dad announced the weight, Eric smiled proudly. Eric's 31-pound 7-ounce striped bass set a new Illinois state record.

FIN FACTS

The Spanish mola, also known as a sunfish, can produce up to 300 million eggs at one time.

THE GIRL WITH A GOLDEN LURE

Luck is only part of 16-year-old Heidi Mason's success. She is a dedicated and skilled angler who holds not one but four world records.

During her first big game fishing trip, Heidi landed a 53-pound sailfish. She was only 7 years old. At age 11, she caught a 308-pound hammerhead shark, and during that same year she released more than 25 sailfish, 11 of which were caught on 8-pound test fishing line.

Credit for releases in the tournaments means much more to Heidi than killing and weighing a fish. Florida's largest fishing tournament, the annual MET (Metropolitan South Florida) tour-

DURING HER FIRST BIG GAME FISHING TRIP, HEIDI LANDED A 53-POUND SAILFISH. SHE WAS ONLY 7 YEARS OLD.

nament, runs five months and includes anglers from around the world. Heidi, since age 11, has won or placed in most of the MET's line and release categories she's fished in, including top angler five out of the last six years.

At age 13, Heidi was awarded Junior Master Angler in the tournament and caught her second world record fish.

"It was toward the end of the MET," Heidi says. "Captain John Dudas had taken me and my father out to try and catch a fish to win the junior overall championship. We decided to go after amberjack and also the category for most releases."

Captain Dudas took Heidi and her dad to a wreck off Biscayne Bay, Florida.

The fishing was good from the start, and the amberjack stayed hungry all day. Heidi had planned to catch and release as many amberjack as she could, and she used heavy tackle with 80-pound test fishing line because of the strong current that day.

"We had been catching amberjack all day," Heidi says. "When the big one hit, my reel screamed! The fish ran straight for the wreck to try and break the line, but Captain Dudas was already moving the boat away, and I was pulling back as hard as I could."

The fish was strong, and Heidi needed all her strength to stop it. The fish pulled powerfully on the line, and each turn of the reel was a struggle. Halfway to the boat was as far as the fish would come before diving back toward the safety of the wreck. Each time it dived, Heidi stopped it. An hour passed before the fish was within gaffing range.

Heidi knew the African pompano was large. She also knew it would give her first place. What she didn't know was that it would set a world record.

"The day after I caught the fish," Heidi says, "I was flipping through the IGFA record book. All of a sudden I looked down and said, 'I caught a world record!' My fish was caught on 8-pound test line and weighed 34 pounds, more than the one in the record book. Luckily we had measured it, weighed it on a certified scale, and had taken lots of pictures for the MET Tournament. The catch was approved."

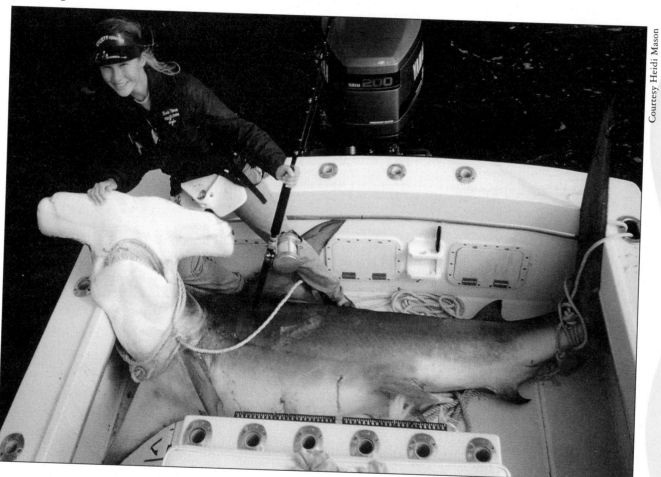

Courtesy Heidi Mason

After fighting this enormous hammerhead for two grueling hours, 15-year-old Heidi Mason landed the 463-pound shark using only 80-pound test line.

The catch qualified for a world record and gave Heidi the Offshore Grand Champion Award for the third year in a row.

Two years later, at age 15, Heidi became the youngest angler in MET tournament history to win the acclaimed Master Angler Award. The tournament began in December 1992 and ran through May 1993. There were more than 20,000 entries, representing 40 different states and 12 foreign countries. Heidi continued her winning streak by winning two more prestigious tournaments in 1994.

It was during the MET Tournament, on April 29, 1993, that Heidi caught her third world record. She fought an enormous hammerhead shark for 2 hours standing up using only a belt-style harness for support. The shark weighed 463 pounds. Earlier that day, she caught a potential fourth world record fish, but a larger fish was caught before her record was approved.

Heidi, however, was not daunted and soon had her fourth world record. It was a 66-pound cobia caught in Miami in February 1995. Heidi hooked and landed the record cobia on 8-pound fishing line after a 3½-hour battle.

"When Heidi was a baby," her mother explains, "we had a huge head mount of a hammerhead shark. It was on the wall next to the changing table, and every time we changed her, she stared up at the shark. I think she was destined to catch fish from then on."

10 WEIRD THINGS FOUND IN THE BELLIES OF SHARKS:

- a suit of armor with a guy inside!
- an alarm clock
- a surfboard
- a wristwatch
- beer cans
- tree trunks
- coal
- license plates
- a man's overcoat
- a nearly whole reindeer